DECLINE AND FALL

BYZANTIUM AT WAR

Written by Richard Bodley Scott, assisted
by Nik Gaukroger, James Hamilton and
Paul Robinson

OSPREY
PUBLISHING

SLITHERINE

First published in Great Britain in 2008 by Osprey Publishing Ltd.

Osprey Publishing, Midland House, West Way, Botley, Oxford OX2 0PH, UK
443 Park Avenue South, New York, NY 10016, USA
E-mail: info@ospreypublishing.com

Slitherine Software UK Ltd., The White Cottage, 8 West Hill Avenue, Epsom, KT 19 8LE, UK
E-mail: info@slitherine.co.uk

A CIP catalogue record for this book is available from the British Library

ISBN: 978 1 84603 402 2

Rules system written by Richard Bodley Scott, Simon Hall, and Terry Shaw
Page layout and cover concept by Myriam Bell
Index by Mike Parkin
Typeset in Joanna Pro and Sleepy Hollow
Cover artwork by Peter Dennis
Photography by Brian O'Dea, Dan Hazelwood, Don McHugh, Essex Miniatures, Neil Hammond,
Philip Knapke & Will Hardiman
Page design features supplied by istockphoto.com
All artwork and cartography © Osprey Publishing Ltd
Project management by JD McNeil and Osprey Team
Technical management by Iain McNeil
Originated by PDQ Media, UK
Printed in China through Worldprint Ltd

08 09 10 11 12   10 9 8 7 6 5 4 3 2 1

FOR A CATALOGUE OF ALL BOOKS PUBLISHED BY OSPREY MILITARY
AND AVIATION PLEASE CONTACT:

NORTH AMERICA
Osprey Direct, c/o Random House Distribution Center, 400 Hahn Road,
Westminster, MD 21157
E-mail: info@ospreydirect.com

ALL OTHER REGIONS
Osprey Direct UK, P.O. Box 140 Wellingborough, Northants, NN8 2FA, UK
E-mail: info@ospreydirect.co.uk

FOR DETAILS OF ALL GAMES PUBLISHED BY SLITHERINE SOFTWARE UK LTD
E-mail: info@slitherine.co.uk

Osprey Publishing is supporting the Woodland Trust, the UK's leading woodland
conservation charity, by funding the dedication of trees.

www.ospreypublishing.com
www.slitherine.com

CONTENTS

INTRODUCTION

This book covers the armies of the Byzantine Empire, the Islamic states and their other enemies, from 493 AD until the mid-11th century.

In 300 AD the Roman Emperor Constantine the Great founded Nova Roma (New Rome) on the site of the existing Greek city of Byzantion. It was to be the new capital of the Roman Empire. After his death it was renamed Konstantinoúpolis (Constantinople).

The last West Roman Emperor, Romulus Augustulus, was deposed by the foederate Odoacer in 476. Odoacer was defeated and replaced by the Ostrogoths in 493. The East Roman Empire persisted. Historians usually call it the Byzantine Empire. As far as its mainly Greek-speaking inhabitants and their contemporary neighbours were concerned, however, it was still the Roman Empire. It lasted until Constantinople fell to the Ottoman Turks in 1453.

From 533–561, in the reign of the Emperor Justinian I, Byzantine armies reconquered North Africa from the Vandals, Italy from the Ostrogoths and Southern Spain from the Visigoths. This was to be the high water mark of the Byzantine Empire.

The Collapse of the West, by Angus McBride. Taken from Men-at-Arms 247: Romano-Byzantine Armies 4th–9th Centuries.

INTRODUCTION

From 602–618, the eastern provinces of the Empire, including Mesopotamia, Syria, Palestine and Egypt, were conquered by the Sassanid Persians, and in 626 Constantinople was besieged by the Avars and their Persian allies. Constantinople held out. By attacking the Persians in their heartland, the Emperor Herakleios won the war and regained the lost eastern provinces. However, large areas of the Empire's European provinces were now occupied by Slavs. More territory south of the Danube was lost to the Bulgars in 679. The Bulgars subsequently conquered many of the former Byzantine territories held by Slavs and these areas were not reconquered by the Byzantines until the turn of the 10th/11th centuries.

In 633, the Arabs, newly united under Islam by Mohammed, erupted from the Arabian peninsula to attack the Byzantines and the Persians, who were both exhausted by their recent war. By 646 the Arabs had wrested Syria, Palestine, Egypt and Mesopotamia from the Byzantines, and by 651 they had conquered most of the Sassanid Persian Empire. Constantinople was besieged unsuccessfully in 674. By 698, the Arabs had captured most of the Byzantine provinces in North Africa. From 711–718 the Visigothic Kingdom in modern Spain fell to invasion. Constantinople was besieged again from 717–718, but once again held out. Further conquests were also made in Central Asia and India, so that by 718, the Umayyad Caliphate ruled a huge Empire stretching from Spain to India.

In 749 rebellion broke out and the Umayyad dynasty was deposed and replaced by the Abbasid dynasty, except in Spain where the Umayyads survived as an independent emirate. Central control declined, however. In 789, the Idrisids formed their own rival Shiite caliphate in Morocco. The Aghlabids in Tunisia achieved de facto independence by about 820. In the east also, new dynasties arose, the Tahirids in 821, Saffarids in 861 and Samanids in 875. These were often only nominally subject to the Abbasid Caliphs. Eqypt became independent under the Tulunids in 868, but was reoccupied by Abbasid troops in 905. From 935 Egypt was held by the Ikhshidid dynasty before being conquered in 969 by the Fatimids from Tunisia. From 946 the Abbasid Caliph became a figurehead only, the remaining territories of the Abbasids (in modern Iraq), including the capital Baghdad, being ruled by the Dailami Buwayhids.

In the middle of the 11th century the Seljuk Turks erupted onto the scene, conquering the Ghaznavids (in modern Afghanistan and Central Asia) and the Buwayhids before attacking the Byzantine Empire. In 1071 they decisively defeated the Byzantines at Manzikert, following which the Byzantines lost most of Asia Minor (modern Turkey). By the end of our period the Byzantine Empire was largely reduced to its European territories, the Seljuk Turks ruled from the Aegean to the borders of India, and the Fatimids controlled Egypt. North-West Africa and Spain were dominated by various independent emirates, though the Christian reconquest of the peninsula was well underway.

EARLY BYZANTINE

This list covers the armies of the Eastern Roman Empire from the final demise of the Western Empire in 493 AD until the widespread adoption of lances for some ranks of the line cavalry c. 550.

FLAVIUS BELISARIUS
(c. 505–565)

Rightly regarded as one of the great generals of history, Belisarius was in large part responsible for the success of the Emperor Justinian I's ambitious plan to reconquer much of the Western Roman Empire from the Goths and Vandals. His achievements were all the more remarkable as they were accomplished despite far from adequate support.

Appointed commander of the Byzantine army in the East by Justinian following his accession in 527, he defeated the Sassanid Persians (see Field of Glory Companion 5: *Legions Triumphant: Imperial Rome at War*) at Dara in 530, but was defeated by them at Nisibis later in the year and Callinicum the following year. Peace was negotiated in 532, with the Byzantines returning captured territory and paying tribute to the Persians, and lasted until 540.

In 532 Belisarius suppressed the Nika riots, a rebellion of the chariot racing factions in Constantinople that nearly deposed Justinian.

From 533–534 Belisarius commanded the Byzantine expedition to recover North Africa

The Byzantine Empire c. AD 550. Taken from Essential Histories 33: Byzantium at War.

from the Vandals. He defeated the Vandals at the battles of Ad Decimum (near Carthage) and Tricamarum. The Vandals surrendered and North Africa was restored to the Empire.

In 535 Justinian dispatched Belisarius against the Ostrogothic Kingdom of Italy. By 536 he had recaptured Rome. In 537 the Goths besieged Belisarius in Rome, but failed to take the city. In 540, Ravenna, the Ostrogothic capital, was captured.

Belisarius was then recalled to the East where he fought an indecisive campaign against the Persians from 541–542. In 544 he returned to Italy, where the Ostrogoths had revived and retaken all of the northern Italy and Rome itself. Starved of reinforcements by Justinian, who was by now worried that Belisarius might try to supplant him, the campaign was not a success. Belisarius went into retirement and Justinian sent the eunuch Narses, with adequate forces, to complete the conquest of Italy, which he did after decisively defeating the Goths at Taginae in 552.

In 559 Belisarius was recalled from retirement to command against a Bulgar invasion that threatened Constantinople itself. He defeated the Bulgars despite being severely outnumbered. In 562, he was imprisoned on trumped up charges of corruption, but was pardoned soon after. He died in 565, within a few weeks of the Emperor Justinian.

TROOP NOTES

While *bucellarii* may or may not all have been double armed with lance and bow, the later Byzantines found it impossible to train all the men in a unit up to the same standard with both weapons. Thus, whether or not all have both weapons, the front rank base is treated as lancers and the back rank base as archers.

After the fall of the Vandal kingdom 5 regiments of *Vandali Justiniani* were formed and sent to the eastern front.

Byzantine Cavalry

EARLY BYZANTINE STARTER ARMY

Commander–in–Chief	1	Inspired Commander (Belisarius)
Sub–commanders	2	2 x Troop Commander
Bucellarii	2 BGs	Each comprising 4 bases of Bucellarii: 2 Superior, Armoured, Drilled Cavalry – Lancers, Swordsmen, 2 Superior, Armoured, Drilled Cavalry – Bow, Swordsmen
Other Roman cavalry	2 BGs	Each comprising 4 bases of other Roman cavalry: Average, Armoured, Drilled Cavalry – Bow, Swordsmen
Moorish cavalry	1 BG	4 bases of Moorish cavalry: Average, Unprotected, Undrilled Light Horse – Javelins, Light Spear
Hunnic cavalry	1 BG	4 bases of Hunnic cavalry: Average, Unprotected, Undrilled Light Horse – Bow, Swordsmen
Legiones or auxilia	2 BGs	Each comprising 9 bases of legiones or auxilia: 6 Average, Protected, Drilled Heavy Foot – Light Spear, Swordsmen, 3 Average, Unprotected, Drilled Light Foot – Bow
Camp	1	Unfortified camp
Total	8 BGs	Camp, 24 mounted bases, 18 foot bases, 3 commanders

Constantinople's Theodosian walls c.AD 447, by Peter Dennis. Taken from Fortress 25: The Walls of Constantinople AD 324–1453.

BUILDING A CUSTOMISED LIST USING OUR ARMY POINTS

Choose an army based on the maxima and minima in the list below. The following special instructions apply to this army:

- Commanders should be depicted as *bucellarii*.
- Gepid, Herul or Lombard cavalry can always dismount as Heavy Foot, Superior, Undrilled, Armoured or Protected (as mounted type), - , Defensive Spearmen.

Byzantine Legionary

Justinian's Army, 6th century, by Angus McBride. Taken from Men-at-Arms 247: Romano-Byzantine Armies 4th–9th Centuries.

EARLY BYZANTINE

Territory Types: Developed, Agricultural, Hilly, Mountains

C−in−C	Inspired Commander/Field Commander/Troop Commander					80/50/35	1	
Sub−commanders	Field Commander					50	0−2	
	Troop Commander					35	0−3	
Troop name	**Troop Type**				**Capabilities**		**Points per base**	**Bases per BG**	**Total bases**
	Type	Armour	Quality	Training	Shooting	Close Combat			
Core Troops									
Bucellarii	Cavalry	Armoured	Superior	Drilled	−	Lancers, Swordsmen	17	1/2	4−6	4−12
	Cavalry	Armoured	Superior	Drilled	Bow	Swordsmen	19	1/2		
Other Roman cavalry	Cavalry	Armoured	Average	Drilled	Bow	Swordsmen	15	4−6	8−24
Legiones or Auxilia	Heavy Foot	Protected	Average	Drilled	−	Light Spear, Swordsmen	7	2/3	6−12	6−36
	Light Foot	Unprotected	Average	Drilled	Bow	−	5	1/3		
	Heavy Foot	Protected	Poor	Drilled	−	Light Spear, Swordsmen	5	2/3	6−12	
	Light Foot	Unprotected	Poor	Drilled	Bow	−	3	1/3		
Optional Troops									
Gepid, Gothic, Herul or Lombard cavalry	Cavalry	Armoured	Superior	Undrilled	−	Lancers, Swordsmen	16	4−6	0−12
		Protected		Undrilled			12		
Vandali Justiniani or similar cavalry	Cavalry	Armoured	Superior	Drilled	−	Lancers, Swordsmen	17	4−6	
		Protected					13		
Moorish cavalry	Light Horse	Unprotected	Average	Undrilled	Javelins	Light Spear	7	4	0−4
Hunnic cavalry	Light Horse	Unprotected	Superior	Undrilled	Bow	Swordsmen	12	4−6	0−8
			Average				10		
	Cavalry	Unprotected	Superior	Undrilled	Bow	Swordsmen	12	4−6	0−8
		Unprotected	Average				10		
		Protected	Superior				14		
		Protected	Average				11		
Archers in separate units	Medium Foot	Unprotected	Average	Drilled	Bow	−	6	6−8	0−8
			Poor				4		
	Light Foot	Unprotected	Average	Drilled	Bow	−	5	6−8	
			Poor				3		
Isaurians or other similar javelinmen	Medium Foot	Protected	Average	Undrilled	−	Light Spear	5	6−8	0−8
	Light Foot	Unprotected	Average	Undrilled	Javelins	Light Spear	4		
Poor quality javelinmen	Medium Foot	Protected	Poor	Undrilled	−	Light Spear	3	6−8	0−8
Other levies	Mob	Unprotected	Poor	Undrilled	−	−	2	6−8	0−8
Field fortifications	Field Fortifications						3		0−12
Fortified camp							24		0−1
Allies									
Arab allies − See Field of Glory Companion 1: *Rise of Rome: Republican Rome at War*									

LATER MOORISH

This list covers Moorish armies from the revolts against the Romans of the mid-4th century AD until the Arab conquest at the end of the 7th century.

BUILDING A CUSTOMISED LIST USING OUR ARMY POINTS

Choose an army based on the maxima and minima in the list below. The following special instructions apply to this army:

- Commanders should be depicted as cavalry.
- Tethered camels are treated as Field Fortifications but disorder cavalry as if camelry, and cost extra points as per camelry.

LATER MOORISH

Territory Types: Agricultural, Hilly, Steppes

C–in–C	Inspired Commander/Field Commander/Troop Commander						80/50/35		1	
Sub–commanders	Field Commander						50		0–2	
	Troop Commander						35		0–3	
Troop name	Troop Type				Capabilities		Points per base	Bases per BG	Total bases	
	Type	Armour	Quality	Training	Shooting	Close Combat				
Core Troops										
Cavalry	Light Horse	Unprotected	Average	Undrilled	Javelins	Light Spear	7	4–6	16–92	
Javelinmen	Light Foot	Unprotected	Average	Undrilled	Javelins	Light Spear	4	6–8	16–112	
Optional Troops										
Archers	Light Foot	Unprotected	Average	Undrilled	Bow	–	5	6–8	0–12	
Slingers	Light Foot	Unprotected	Average	Undrilled	Sling	–	4	6–8		
Families	Mob	Unprotected	Poor	Undrilled	–	–	2	8–12	0–12	
Tethered camels	Field Fortifications						5		0–24	
Special Campaigns										
Only from 533 to 548										
Vandal refugees	Cavalry	Armoured	Superior	Undrilled	–	Lancers, Swordsmen	16	4–6	0–6	
Byzantine deserters	Cavalry	Armoured	Average	Drilled	Bow	Swordsmen	15	4–6	0–6	

LATER MOORISH ALLIES

Allied commander	Field Commander/Troop Commander						40/25		1	
Troop name	Troop Type				Capabilities		Points per base	Bases per BG	Total bases	
	Type	Armour	Quality	Training	Shooting	Close Combat				
Cavalry	Light Horse	Unprotected	Average	Undrilled	Javelins	Light Spear	7	4–6	4–18	
Javelinmen	Light Foot	Unprotected	Average	Undrilled	Javelins	Light Spear	4	6–8	6–24	

Moorish warriors, by Angus McBride. Taken from Men-at-Arms 348: The Moors.

LATER VISIGOTHIC

In 418 AD, following their campaign, at Roman instigation, against the Vandals, Alans and Suebi in the Iberian peninsula (modern Spain), the Visigoths were rewarded with land in Gallia Aquitania (modern south-west France). By 475 the kingdom had achieved full independence. By 500, it had extended its territory to include most of modern southern France and much of Spain.

In 507, however, the Visigoths were defeated by the Franks and lost most of their territory in the north. The capital was moved first to Barcelona, then to Toledo.

In 554, the Byzantines reoccupied the south of the Iberian peninsula after being called in to help one side in a Visigothic civil war. In 585, the Visigoths conquered the Suebi kingdom in the north-west and incorporated it into their territory. The south was reconquered from the Byzantines by 624.

In 711 King Roderic (Rodrigo) was defeated and killed at the Battle of Guadalete by the invading Umayyad Muslims under the command of Tariq ibn Ziyad. The Muslims soon conquered the whole of the Iberian peninsula apart from a small strip in the north.

This list covers the Visigothic Kingdom from 419 until the completion of the Arab conquest c.718.

LATER VISIGOTHIC STARTER ARMY		
Commander–in–Chief	1	Field Commander
Sub–commanders	2	2 x Troop Commander
Bucellarii	2 BGs	Each comprising 4 bases of Bucellarii: Superior, Armoured, Undrilled Cavalry – Lancers, Swordsmen
Gardingi	2 BGs	Each comprising 4 bases of Gardingi: Superior, Protected, Undrilled Cavalry – Light Spear, Swordsmen
Basque cavalry	1 BG	4 bases of Basque cavalry: Average, Unprotected, Undrilled Light Horse – Javelins, Light Spear
Spearmen	3 BGs	Each comprising 8 bases of spearmen: Average, Protected, Undrilled Heavy Foot – Defensive Spearmen
Archers	2 BGs	Each comprising 8 bases of archers: Average, Unprotected, Undrilled Light Foot – Bow
Camp	1	Unfortified camp
Total	10 BGs	Camp, 20 mounted bases, 40 foot bases, 3 commanders

BUILDING A CUSTOMISED LIST USING OUR ARMY POINTS

Choose an army based on the maxima and minima in the list below. The following special instructions apply to this army:

- Commanders should be depicted as *bucellarii*.
- Only one allied contingent can be used.

LATER VISIGOTHIC

Territory Types: Agricultural, Developed, Hilly, Woodlands (only before 507), Mountains (only from 507)

C–in–C		Inspired Commander/Field Commander/Troop Commander					80/50/35		1	
Sub–commanders		Field Commander					50		0–2	
		Troop Commander					35		0–3	
Troop name		Troop Type				Capabilities		Points per base	Bases per BG	Total bases
		Type	Armour	Quality	Training	Shooting	Close Combat			
Core Troops										
Bucellarii		Cavalry	Armoured	Superior	Undrilled	–	Lancers, Swordsmen	16	4–6	4–12
Gardingi		Cavalry	Protected	Superior	Undrilled	–	Light Spear, Swordsmen	12	4–6	6–30
				Average				9		
Spearmen	Only before 622	Heavy Foot	Protected	Average	Undrilled	–	Impact foot, Swordsmen	7	8–12	8–72
Spearmen	Only from 622	Heavy Foot	Protected	Average	Undrilled	–	Defensive Spearmen	6	2/3 or all	8–72
Supporting archers		Light Foot	Unprotected	Average	Undrilled	Bow	–	5	1/3 or 0	0–24
Separately deployed archers		Light Foot	Unprotected	Average	Undrilled	Bow	–	5	6–8	0–24
		Medium Foot	Unprotected	Average	Undrilled	Bow	–	5	6–8	6–24
Optional Troops										
Romans	Before 467	Heavy or Medium Foot	Protected	Poor	Drilled	–	Light Spear, Swordsmen	5	2/3 or all	0–18
		Light Foot	Unprotected	Poor	Drilled	Bow	–	3	1/3 or 0	
	From 467	Heavy Foot	Protected	Poor	Undrilled	–	Defensive Spearmen	4	2/3 or all	0–18
		Light Foot	Unprotected	Poor	Undrilled	Bow	–	3	1/3 or 0	
Slingers		Light Foot	Unprotected	Average	Undrilled	Sling	–	4	4–6	0–6
Basque cavalry	Only from 622	Light Horse	Unprotected	Average	Undrilled	Javelins	Light Spear	7	4	0–4
Basque javelinmen	Only from 622	Light Foot	Unprotected	Average	Undrilled	Javelins	Light Spear	4	4–8	0–8
Fortified camp								24		0–1
Allies										

Only before 467

Burgundian allies – Early Frankish, Alamanni, Burgundi, Limigantes, Rugian, Suebi or Turcilingi – See Field of Glory Companion 5: *Legions Triumphant: Imperial Rome at War*

Only from 467 to 621

Byzantine allies – Maurikian Byzantine (550 to 554)

Ostrogothic allies – Italian Ostrogothic

Suebi allies – Early Frankish, Alamanni, Burgundi, Limigantes, Rugian, Suebi or Turcilingi – See Field of Glory Companion 5: *Legions Triumphant: Imperial Rome at War*

LATER VISIGOTHIC ALLIES

Allied commander		Field Commander/Troop Commander						40/25		1	
Troop name		**Troop Type**				**Capabilities**		**Points per base**	**Bases per BG**	**Total bases**	
		Type	Armour	Quality	Training	Shooting	Close Combat				
Bucellarii		Cavalry	Armoured	Superior	Undrilled	–	Lancers, Swordsmen	16	4	0–4	
Gardingi		Cavalry	Protected	Superior	Undrilled	–	Light Spear, Swordsmen	12	4–6	4–8	
				Average				9			
Spearmen	Only before 622	Heavy Foot	Protected	Average	Undrilled	–	Impact foot, Swordsmen	7	8–12	0–24	
Spearmen	Only from 622	Heavy Foot	Protected	Average	Undrilled	–	Defensive Spearmen	6	2/3 or all	8–12	0–24
Supporting archers		Light Foot	Unprotected	Average	Undrilled	Bow	–	5	1/3 or 0	0–8	0–8
Separately deployed archers		Light Foot	Unprotected	Average	Undrilled	Bow	–	5	6–8	0–8	0–8
		Medium Foot	Unprotected	Average	Undrilled	Bow	–	5	6–8		

AFRICAN VANDAL

In 429 AD, political machinations in the Roman high command led to the Roman commander in North Africa, Boniface, inviting the Vandals under King Geiseric to cross over from modern Spain to Africa to aid him against the central government. Once there they could not be dislodged. By 439 they had captured Carthage itself and made it the capital of their new kingdom. In 442 the Romans, in order to secure the corn supply from Africa, recognised the status quo.

As "King of the Vandals and Alans", Geiseric used his large fleet to conquer Sardinia, Corsica, the Balearic Islands and the western end of Sicily, and to pillage at will the coasts of the Mediterranean. In 455 the Vandals sacked Rome itself. In 468 they defeated a large East Roman fleet sent against them, then failed in an attempt to invade southern Greece. On the way back to Carthage they slaughtered 500 hostages and threw them overboard. Despite this, a peace treaty was concluded in 476.

In 533 the Byzantines invaded under the command of Belisarius. The Vandals were defeated at the Battles of Ad Decimum and Tricamarum. In 534 King Gelimer surrendered to the Byzantines, thus ending the Vandal Kingdom. The surviving Vandal men were enslaved or recruited into the Byzantine army. Five cavalry regiments, known as *Vandali Iustiniani*, were formed and sent to the Persian frontier. The Vandal womenfolk married Byzantine soldiers. Gelimer was granted large estates in Galatia to which he retired.

This list covers Vandal armies from 442 until 534.

Vandal Cavalry

BUILDING A CUSTOMISED LIST USING OUR ARMY POINTS

Choose an army based on the maxima and minima in the list below. The following special instructions apply to this army:

- Commanders should be depicted as Vandal cavalry.

AFRICAN VANDAL									
Territory Types: Agricultural									
C–in–C	Inspired Commander/Field Commander/Troop Commander						80/50/35		1
Sub–commanders	Field Commander						50		0–2
	Troop Commander						35		0–3
Troop name	Troop Type				Capabilities		Points per base	Bases per BG	Total bases
	Type	Armour	Quality	Training	Shooting	Close Combat			
Core Troops									
Vandal cavalry	Cavalry	Armoured	Superior	Undrilled	–	Lancers, Swordsmen	16	4–6	12–68
Optional Troops									
Moorish cavalry	Light Horse	Unprotected	Average	Undrilled	Javelins	Light Spear	7	4	0–4
Alans Only before 500	Light Horse	Unprotected	Average	Undrilled	Bow	Swordsmen	10	4–6	0–6
	Cavalry	Unprotected	Average	Undrilled	Bow	Swordsmen	10	4–6	
		Protected					11		
Fortified camp							24		0–1
Allies									
Moorish allies (Only before 500) – Later Moorish									

ITALIAN OSTROGOTHIC

In 488, under King Theodoric the Great, the Ostrogoths set out, at the request of the Eastern Roman Emperor Zeno, to conquer Italy from King Odoacer – the Sciri foederate who had deposed the last Western Roman Emperor in 476. By 493 Odoacer was defeated and killed and Theoderic became King of Italy, ruling modern Italy, Slovenia, Croatia and Bosnia.

In theory he acted as viceroy for the Roman Emperor in Constantinople, and he scrupulously observed the outward forms of this, but in reality he was an entirely independent ruler. The Goths, who were mostly settled in the north, largely kept separate from the native population, were subject to Gothic law and formed the army of the kingdom. The civil administration, however, was staffed by Romans, the Senate functioned as before, and the native population continued to be subject to Roman law.

Theoderic also exercised dominance over the Visigothic Kingdom in modern southern France and Spain. When the Visigoths were defeated by the

Ostrogoth Cavalryman

Franks in 507, the Ostrogothic army campaigned against the Franks and managed to save a coastal strip for the the the Visigoths as well as gaining control of Provence for themselves. Theoderic died in 526.

In 535, the Byzantine Emperor Justinian sent an invasion force under Belisarius. This was initially successful, the Gothic capital Ravenna fell in 540, and the kingdom was ostensibly conquered, apart from Ticinum and Verona, north of the Po. Following the recall of Belisarius to command against a new attack by the Sassanid Persians in the East, however, the Goths began to recover, aided by the lack of cooperation between the Byzantine generals left in Italy. Under King Totila, the Goths defeated several Roman forces and regained much of the kingdom.

Belisarius returned in 544, but with inadequate forces he was unable to achieve any great success. Justinian then sent the eunuch Narses with larger forces. The Goths were defeated at Taginae in 552 and Mons Lactarius in 553.

This list covers the Ostrogothic kingdom from the defeat of Odoacer in 493 until the final completion of the Byzantine reconquest in 561. The Byzantines did not enjoy their victory for long. In 568 the Lombards invaded and conquered more than half of Italy.

ITALIAN OSTROGOTHIC STARTER ARMY		
Commander–in–Chief	1	Field Commander
Sub–commanders	2	2 x Troop Commander
Cavalry	4 BGs	Each comprising 4 bases of cavalry: Superior, Armoured, Undrilled Cavalry – Lancers, Swordsmen
Huns	1 BG	4 bases of Huns: Average, Unprotected, Undrilled Light Horse – Bow, Swordsmen
Spearmen	2 BGs	Each comprising 8 bases of spearmen: Average, Protected, Undrilled Heavy Foot – Defensive Spearmen
Archers	2 BGs	Each comprising 8 bases of archers: Average, Unprotected, Undrilled Light Foot – Bow
Levies	1 BG	4 bases of levies: Poor, Unprotected, Undrilled Mob – No capabilities
Camp	1	Unfortified camp
Total	10 BGs	Camp, 20 mounted bases, 36 foot bases, 3 commanders

BUILDING A CUSTOMISED LIST USING OUR ARMY POINTS

Choose an army based on the maxima and minima in the list below. The following special instructions apply to this army:

• Commanders should be depicted as cavalry.

ITALIAN OSTROGOTHIC

Territory Types: Developed, Agricultural, Hilly

C–in–C		Inspired Commander/Field Commander/Troop Commander					80/50/35		1	
Sub–commanders		Field Commander					50		0–2	
		Troop Commander					35		0–3	
Troop name		Troop Type				Capabilities		Points per base	Bases per BG	Total bases
	Type	Armour	Quality	Training	Shooting	Close Combat				
Core Troops										
Cavalry	Cavalry	Armoured	Superior	Undrilled	–	Lancers, Swordsmen		16	4–6	12–50
Spearmen	Heavy Foot	Protected	Average	Undrilled	–	Defensive Spearmen		6	2/3 or all	0–16
Supporting archers	Light Foot	Unprotected	Average	Undrilled	Bow	–		5	1/3 or 0	0–8
Separately deployed archers	Light Foot	Unprotected	Average	Undrilled	Bow	–		5	6–8	12–36
	Medium Foot	Unprotected	Average	Undrilled	Bow	–		5	6–8	
Optional Troops										
Huns	Light Horse	Unprotected	Superior	Undrilled	Bow	Swordsmen		12	4	0–4
			Average					10		
	Cavalry	Unprotected	Superior	Undrilled	Bow	Swordsmen		12	4	
		Unprotected	Average					10		
		Protected	Superior					14		
		Protected	Average					11		
Upgrade separately deployed archers with mantlets to:	Medium Foot	Protected	Average	Undrilled	Bow	–		6	6–8	0–8
Levies	Mob	Unprotected	Poor	Undrilled	–	–		2	4–6	0–6
Fortified camp								24		0–1
Allies										
Burgundian allies – Early Frankish, Alamanni, Burgundi, Limigantes, Rugian, Suebi or Turcilingi or Middle Frankish – See Field of Glory Companion 5: *Legions Triumphant: Imperial Rome at War*										
Frankish allies (Only after 548) – Middle Frankish – See Field of Glory Companion 8: *Wolves From the Sea: The Dark Ages*										
Special campaigns										
Only from 544 to 552										
Byzantine deserters	Cavalry	Armoured	Average	Drilled	Bow	Swordsmen		15	4	0–4

EARLY SOUTH SLAV

The Slavic tribes of the Venets, the Antes and the Sklavens (Sklavinoi) first appear in Byzantine records in the early 6th century AD, invading the Danubian provinces of the Empire. By the end of their migratory movements, Slavic territory included most of the former Yugoslavia, the interior of central Greece and even much of the Peloponnese.

The Serbs entered modern Serbia in the early 7th century, one of their first states being Raška, which eventually became a kingdom in 1217 and the Serbian Empire in 1346.

The Croats also arrived in modern Croatia in the 7th century, initially forming two dukedoms, which were combined into a kingdom in the 10th century. After the defeat and death in 1097 of the last Croatian king, Petar Svačić, at the Battle of Gvozd Mountain against King Coloman I of Hungary, Croatia accepted dynastic union with Hungary under King Coloman in 1102. This lasted until 1918.

The Serbs and Croats may have been of Sarmatian origin, but after arriving in the region rapidly assimilated with their Slav subjects.

This list covers the South Slav armies from the 6th century until the 12th century AD.

BUILDING A CUSTOMISED LIST USING OUR ARMY POINTS

Choose an army based on the maxima and minima in the list below. The following special instructions apply to this army:

- Commanders should be depicted as noble cavalry.
- Croatian noble cavalry can either have lancers or light spear close combat capability, but all must have the same capability.

EARLY SOUTH SLAV

Territory Types: Hilly, Woodlands

Troop name		Troop Type				Capabilities		Points per base	Bases per BG	Total bases
		Type	Armour	Quality	Training	Shooting	Close Combat			
C–in–C		Inspired Commander/Field Commander/Troop Commander						80/50/35		1
Sub–commanders		Field Commander						50	0–2	
		Troop Commander						35	0–3	
Core Troops										
Noble cavalry	Serbians	Cavalry	Protected	Superior	Undrilled	–	Lancers, Swordsmen	12	4–6	4–24
			Armoured					16		
	Croatians	Cavalry	Protected	Superior	Undrilled	–	Lancers, Swordsmen	12	4–6	4–20
			Armoured					16		
		Cavalry	Protected	Superior	Undrilled	–	Light Spear, Swordsmen	12		
			Armoured					16		
	Others	Cavalry	Protected	Superior	Undrilled	–	Light Spear, Swordsmen	12	4–6	4–16
			Armoured					16		
Foot warriors	Before 850	Medium Foot	Protected	Average	Undrilled	–	Light Spear	5	6–8	24–136
	From 850	Heavy Foot	Protected	Average	Undrilled	–	Defensive Spearmen	6	6–8	12–120
				Poor				4		
Archers	Serbians	Medium Foot	Unprotected	Average	Undrilled	Bow	–	5	6–8	8–32
		Light Foot	Unprotected	Average	Undrilled	Bow	–	5	6–8	
	Others	Light Foot	Unprotected	Average	Undrilled	Bow	–	5	6–8	0–16
Optional Troops										
Skirmishing javelinmen		Light Foot	Unprotected	Average	Undrilled	Javelins	Light Spear	4	6–8	0–16
Poorly armed foot		Medium Foot	Unprotected	Poor	Undrilled	–	Light Spear	2	8–12	0–36

EARLY SOUTH SLAV ALLIES

Allied commander			Field Commander/Troop Commander				40/25		1
Troop name		**Troop Type**				**Capabilities**		**Points per base**	**Bases per BG**	**Total bases**
		Type	Armour	Quality	Training	Shooting	Close Combat			
Noble cavalry	Serbians	Cavalry	Protected	Superior	Undrilled	–	Lancers, Swordsmen	12	4–6	0–6
			Armoured					16		
	Croatians	Cavalry	Protected	Superior	Undrilled	–	Lancers, Swordsmen	12	4–6	
			Armoured					16		
		Cavalry	Protected	Superior	Undrilled	–	Light Spear, Swordsmen	12		
			Armoured					16		
	Others	Cavalry	Protected	Superior	Undrilled	–	Light Spear, Swordsmen	12	4–6	
			Armoured					16		
Foot warriors	Before 850	Medium Foot	Protected	Average	Undrilled	–	Light Spear	5	6–8	8–36
	From 850	Heavy Foot	Protected	Average	Undrilled	–	Defensive Spearmen	6	6–8	6–24
				Poor				4		
Archers	Serbians	Medium Foot	Unprotected	Average	Undrilled	Bow	–	5	4–8	4–12
		Light Foot	Unprotected	Average	Undrilled	Bow	–	5	4–6	
	Others	Light Foot	Unprotected	Average	Undrilled	Bow	–	5	4–6	0–6
Skirmishing javelinmen		Light Foot	Unprotected	Average	Undrilled	Javelins	Light Spear	4	4–6	0–6

LOMBARD

In 568 AD, the Lombards, under King Alboin, invaded Italy. The invasion force also included Bavarians, Saxons, Suebi, Gepids and Bulgars. The country had not yet recovered from the Gothic wars, and the Byzantine forces were inadequate to defend it against this horde. The Lombards swiftly conquered northern Italy, creating a Lombard kingdom there, with its capital at Pavia. They also pressed on into central and southern Italy, forming the Lombard duchies of Spoleto and Benevento, which soon became semi-independent.

The Byzantines retained control of a narrow corridor from Ravenna to Rome (between the Lombard Kingdom and the Duchies of Spoleto and Benevento), Calabria (the toe of Italy), part of Apulia (the heel of Italy) and Sicily. Together, the mainland territories formed the Exarchate of Ravenna.

Ravenna fell to the Lombards in 751. In 754 the Pope called in the Frankish King Pepin III, who defeated the Lombards and drove them out of the exarchate. In 756, accepting the forged "Donation of Constantine" at face value, Pepin recognised the Pope's right to rule over the central Italian territories of the Exarchate of Ravenna, thus creating the Papal States.

The Lombards went back on the offensive, recaptured Ravenna, and, in 772, captured Rome. The Pope, Hadrian I, appealed for help to the great Frankish king Charlemagne, who invaded in 773 and had conquered the Lombard Kingdom by 774, taking the title "King of the Lombards". In 776 the Duchy of Spoleto also fell.

The Lombard Duchy of Benevento, under Duke Arechis II, remained independent. Arechis declared himself Prince, although he was forced to accept Frankish rule in 787. In the mid-9th century, the Principality was divided into the Principalities of Benevento, Salerno and Capua.

Despite attacks by the Franks, the Byzantines and later the Holy Roman Emperor, the Lombard principalities survived until finally conquered by the Normans under Robert Guiscard between 1053 and 1077.

This list covers independent Lombard armies from 568 until 1077.

TROOP NOTES

Early Lombard armies formed up in two lines, the first of armoured cavalry, the second of unarmoured followers.

BUILDING A CUSTOMISED LIST USING OUR ARMY POINTS

Choose an army based on the maxima and minima in the list below. The following special instructions apply to this army:

- Commanders should be depicted as armoured cavalry.
- Bavarians, Bulgars, Gepids, Old Saxons or Suebi can be used together, otherwise only one allied contingent can be used.

LOMBARD

Territory Types: Developed, Agricultural, Hilly

C–in–C		Inspired Commander/Field Commander/Troop Commander						80/50/35		1	
Sub–commanders		Field Commander						50		0–2	
		Troop Commander						35		0–3	
Troop name		Troop Type				Capabilities		Points per base	Bases per BG	Total bases	
		Type	Armour	Quality	Training	Shooting	Close Combat				
Core Troops											
Armoured cavalry		Cavalry	Armoured	Superior	Undrilled	–	Lancers, Swordsmen	16	4–6	6–56	12–68
Separately deployed unarmoured followers	Only before 776	Cavalry	Protected	Average	Undrilled	–	Lancers, Swordsmen	9	4–6	6–36	
			Unprotected					8			
Archers		Medium Foot	Unprotected	Average	Undrilled	Bow	–	5	6–8	6–24	
				Poor				3			
		Light Foot	Unprotected	Average	Undrilled	Bow	–	5	6–8		
				Poor				3			
Italian militias	Only from 650	Heavy Foot	Protected	Poor	Undrilled	–	Defensive Spearmen	4	6–8	6–32	
					Drilled			5			
Optional Troops											
Bulgar or Magyar mercenaries	Only from 650	Light Horse	Unprotected	Average	Undrilled	Bow	Swordsmen	10	4	0–4	
		Cavalry	Unprotected	Average	Undrilled	Bow	Swordsmen	10			
			Protected					11			
Poorly armed foot		Mob	Unprotected	Poor	Undrilled	–	–	2	8–12	0–12	

Allies
Only before 650
Avar allies
Bavarian or Old Saxon allies – Early Anglo–Saxon, Bavarian, Frisian, Old Saxon or Thuringian – See Field of Glory Companion 5: *Legions Triumphant: Imperial Rome at War*
Bulgar allies – Early Bulgar
Gepid subject allies – Gepid or Early Lombard – See Field of Glory Companion 5: *Legions Triumphant: Imperial Rome at War*
Slav allies – Early South Slav (not Serbian or Croatian)
Suebi subject allies – Early Frankish, Alamanni, Burgundi, Limiganti, Rugian, Suebi or Turcilingi – See Field of Glory Companion 5: *Legions Triumphant: Imperial Rome at War*
Only from 776
Aghlabid allies – Early North African Dynasties
Imperialist allies – Carolingian Frankish or Early Medieval German – See Field of Glory Companion 8: *Wolves From the Sea: The Dark Ages*
Norman allies – Italo-Norman – See Note p.78

MAURIKIAN BYZANTINE

By 555 AD, the Emperor Justinian's ambitious project to reconquer the Western Roman Empire from the Germanic tribes had reached its fullest success – Africa, Italy, Illyricum and the south of modern Spain were back under Byzantine control. Justinian and his great general, Belisarius, both died in 565.

In 568, the majority of Italy was conquered by the Lombards (See p.20). The Byzantine possessions in Spain were reduced by the Visigoths to a narrow coastal strip by 575, and finally lost altogether by 624.

The Emperor Maurikios (582–602) codified current Byzantine military practice in the *Strategikon*, a military manual written either by himself or by one of his close circle.

The deposition and murder of Maurikios by Phokas (602–610) formed the pretext for a Sassanid Persian invasion by Khosrau II. The eastern provinces of the Empire, including Mesopotamia, Syria, Palestine and Egypt, were quickly conquered, and, in 626, Constantinople was besieged on the Asian side by the Persians and on the European side by their allies, the Avars. However, the walls of Constantinople were strong, and the Emperor Herakleios (610–641) adopted the strategic master-stroke of sailing up the Black Sea to attack Persia from the rear. Herakleios's campaign into the Persian heartland destroyed Persian morale, already sapped by the long war. Khosrau II was assassinated in 628 and the lost provinces were restored to the Empire. By then, however, most of the former Yugoslavia, the interior of central Greece and even much of the Peloponnese had been lost to the Slavs.

From 634, the Arabs, newly united by Mohammed, invaded and conquered Syria, Palestine, Egypt and Mesopotamia from the Byzantines by 646. These provinces were never to be recaptured.

This list covers Byzantine armies from the widespread adoption of lances for some ranks of the line cavalry c.550 until the completion of the Thematic system (See p.38) c.650.

TROOP NOTES

Byzantine organisation of this period is described in the *Strategikon* of the Emperor Maurikios. Although the ideal was for all ranks of the cavalry to be armed with lance and bow, it was soon

Byzantine commander and bodyguard, by Angus McBride. Taken from Men-at-Arms 247: Romano-Byzantine Armies 4th–9th Centuries.

found impossible to train all the men up to the same standard with both weapons. Thus, whether or not all men in a battle group have both weapons, the front rank base is treated as lancers and the back rank base as archers. The rear rank archers are treated as the same armour class as the lancers, even though they may sometimes have had less armour. When detached, however, they are graded according to their own true armour class.

Though *Phoideratoi* and *Optimates* were both elite units recruited largely from Goths, the former were armed in Byzantine fashion, the latter in Gothic fashion.

The heavy foot normally formed up with long spear and large shield, either 16, 8 or 4 ranks deep with their attached archers either behind or within the files. For fighting in wooded regions, rough terrain and narrow passes they were re-equipped with short spear and medium sized shield.

Byzantine Javelinman

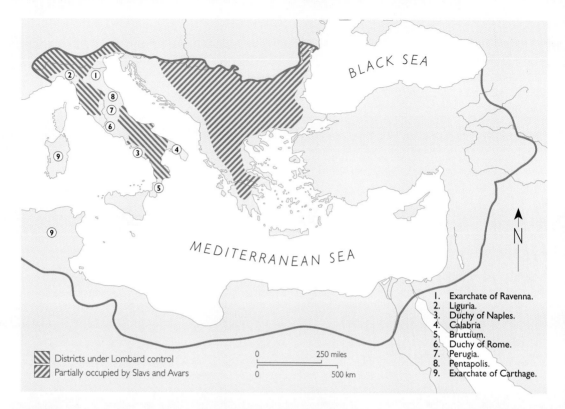

The Byzantine Empire c. AD 600. Taken from Essential Histories 33: Byzantium at War.

Map legend:
- Districts under Lombard control
- Partially occupied by Slavs and Avars

1. Exarchate of Ravenna.
2. Liguria.
3. Duchy of Naples.
4. Calabria
5. Bruttium.
6. Duchy of Rome.
7. Perugia.
8. Pentapolis.
9. Exarchate of Carthage.

MAURIKIAN BYZANTINE STARTER ARMY		
Commander–in–Chief	1	Field Commander
Sub–commanders	2	2 x Troop Commander
Elite cavalry	2 BGs	Each comprising 4 bases of elite cavalry: Superior, Armoured, Drilled Cavalry – 2 Lancers, Swordsmen, 2 Bow, Swordsmen
Line cavalry	2 BGs	Each comprising 4 bases of line cavalry: Average, Armoured, Drilled Cavalry – 2 Lancers, Swordsmen, 2 Bow, Swordsmen
Detached Koursores	1 BG	4 bases of Koursores: Superior, Armoured, Drilled Cavalry – Bow, Swordsmen
Skoutatoi and attached archers	2 BGs	Each comprising 8 bases of skoutatoi and attached archers: 6 Average, Protected, Drilled Heavy Foot – Defensive Spearmen, 2 Average, Unprotected, Drilled Light Foot – Bow
Archers in separate units	1 BG	8 bases of archers: Average, Unprotected, Drilled Light Foot – Bow
Camp	1	Unfortified camp
Total	8 BGs	Camp, 20 mounted bases, 24 foot bases, 3 commanders

MAURIKIAN BYZANTINE

BUILDING A CUSTOMISED LIST USING OUR ARMY POINTS

Choose an army based on the maxima and minima in the list below. The following special instructions apply to this army:

- Commanders should be depicted as elite cavalry.
- The minimum marked * applies if any foot are used.
- Moorish allies cannot be used with any other allies.
- Khazar allies cannot be used with Sassanids.

Troop name	Type	Armour	Quality	Training	Shooting	Close Combat	Points per base	Bases per BG		Total bases

Territory Types: Developed, Agricultural, Hilly, Mountains

C–in–C	Inspired Commander/Field Commander/Troop Commander						80/50/35	1		
Sub–commanders	Field Commander						50	0–2		
	Troop Commander						35	0–3		

Core Troops

Elite cavalry	Cavalry	Armoured	Superior	Drilled	–	Lancers, Swordsmen	17	1/2	4–6	4–12
	Cavalry	Armoured	Superior	Drilled	Bow	Swordsmen	19	1/2		
Optimates	Cavalry	Armoured	Superior	Undrilled	–	Lancers, Swordsmen	16	4–6		0–6
				Drilled			17			
Line cavalry	Cavalry	Armoured	Average	Drilled	–	Lancers, Swordsmen	13	1/2	4–6	8–24
	Cavalry	Armoured	Average	Drilled	Bow	Swordsmen	15	1/2		
Detached Koursores	Cavalry	Armoured	Superior	Drilled	Bow	Swordsmen	19	4–6		0–1 per 2 elite cavalry
	Cavalry	Armoured / Protected	Average	Drilled	Bow	Swordsmen	15 / 12	4–6		0–1 per 2 line cavalry
Skoutatoi and attached archers	Heavy Foot	Protected	Average	Drilled	–	Defensive Spearmen	7	3/4	8–12	*8–24
	Medium Foot	Protected	Average	Drilled	–	Light Spear, Swordsmen	7			
	Light Foot	Unprotected	Average	Drilled	Bow	–	5	1/4		
	Heavy Foot	Protected	Poor	Drilled	–	Defensive Spearmen	5	3/4	8–12	
	Medium Foot	Protected	Poor	Drilled	–	Light Spear, Swordsmen	5			
	Light Foot	Unprotected	Poor	Drilled	Bow	–	3	1/4		
Archers in separate units	Medium Foot	Unprotected	Average / Poor	Drilled	Bow	–	6 / 4	6–8		0–8
	Light Foot	Unprotected	Average / Poor	Drilled	Bow	–	5 / 3	6–8		

Optional Troops

Javelinmen	Medium Foot	Protected	Average	Undrilled	–	Light Spear	5	6–8		0–8
	Light Foot	Unprotected	Average	Undrilled	Javelins	Light Spear	4	6–8		
Bolt–shooters	Heavy Artillery	–	Average	–	Heavy Artillery	–	20	2		0–2
Fortified camp							24			0–1

Allies

Arab allies – See Field of Glory Companion 1: Rise of Rome: Republican Rome at War

Khazar allies – Western Turkish

Moorish allies – Later Moorish

Sassanid allies – See Field of Glory Companion 5: Legions Triumphant: Imperial Rome at War

MAURIKIAN BYZANTINE ALLIES

Allied commander	Field Commander/Troop Commander						40/25		1	
Troop name	**Troop Type**				**Capabilities**		**Points per base**	**Bases per BG**		**Total bases**
	Type	Armour	Quality	Training	Shooting	Close Combat				
Elite cavalry	Cavalry	Armoured	Superior	Drilled	–	Lancers, Swordsmen	17	1/2	4	0–4
	Cavalry	Armoured	Superior	Drilled	Bow	Swordsmen	19	1/2		
Line cavalry	Cavalry	Armoured	Average	Drilled	–	Lancers, Swordsmen	13	1/2	4–6	4–8
	Cavalry	Armoured	Average	Drilled	Bow	Swordsmen	15	1/2		
Detached Koursores	Cavalry	Armoured	Average	Drilled	Bow	Swordsmen	15	4–6		0–1 per 2 elite and line cavalry
		Protected					12			
Skoutatoi	Heavy Foot	Protected	Average	Drilled	–	Defensive Spearmen	7	3/4	8	
	Medium Foot	Protected	Average	Drilled	–	Light Spear, Swordsmen	7			
Attached archers	Light Foot	Unprotected	Average	Drilled	Bow	–	5	1/4		0–8
Skoutatoi	Heavy Foot	Protected	Poor	Drilled	–	Defensive Spearmen	5	3/4	8	
	Medium Foot	Protected	Poor	Drilled	–	Light Spear, Swordsmen	5			
Attached archers	Light Foot	Unprotected	Poor	Drilled	Bow	–	3	1/4		
Archers in separate units	Medium Foot	Unprotected	Average	Drilled	Bow	–	6	4		0–4
			Poor				4			
	Light Foot	Unprotected	Average	Drilled	Bow	–	5	4		
			Poor				3			

CHRISTIAN NUBIAN

This list covers the armies of the Nubian kingdoms of Nobatia, Makouria and Alwa from the conversion of Nobatia to Christianity around 550 AD until the collapse of the kingdom of Alwa c.1500.

The Nubians were the first opponents of the Muslim Arabs that inflicted a major defeat on them (at Dongola in 641 or 642). The Nubians' victory was attributed to their skill as archers. As a result of a second battle in 652, also at Dongola, a peace treaty, known as the Baqt, was agreed whereby the Nubians would pay a tribute including 360 slaves annually to the Arabs.

Despite the Baqt treaty there were still occasional wars between the Nubians and the various Muslim states of Egypt down to Mamluk times, with the Nubians usually coming off second best.

TROOP NOTES

Arab accounts of Nubian armies make no mention of infantry other than the archers, however, there are depictions of spear armed infantry and archaeological finds of substantial spears which indicate that other infantry existed although probably of poorer quality than the archers.

Camel mounted warriors are described as poorly armoured or naked and fighting with spears. Some were Nubians whilst others were Beja nomads. They were routed with ease by Arab cavalry who, on one occasion, tied bells to their horses to frighten the camels.

CHRISTIAN NUBIAN STARTER ARMY

Commander–in–Chief	1	Field Commander
Sub–commanders	2	2 x Troop Commander
Noble cavalry	1 BG	4 bases of noble cavalry: Superior, Armoured, Undrilled Cavalry – Lancers, Swordsmen
Nubian cavalry	2 BGs	Each comprising 4 bases of Nubian cavalry: Average, Unprotected, Undrilled Light Horse – Javelins, Light Spear
Nubian or Beja camel riders	2 BGs	Each comprising 4 bases of Nubian or Beja camel riders: Average, Protected, Undrilled Camelry – Light Spear
Archers	2 BGs	Each comprising 8 bases of archers: Superior, Unprotected, Undrilled Medium Foot – Bow
Archers	3 BGs	Each comprising 8 bases of archers: Average, Unprotected, Undrilled Light Foot – Bow
Spearmen	2 BGs	Each comprising 8 bases of spearmen: Poor, Protected, Undrilled Medium Foot – Defensive Spearmen
Camp	1	Unfortified camp
Total	12 BGs	Camp, 20 mounted bases, 56 foot bases, 3 commanders

BUILDING A CUSTOMISED LIST USING OUR ARMY POINTS

Choose an army based on the maxima and minima in the list below. The following special instructions apply to this army:

- Commanders should be depicted as noble cavalry.

CHRISTIAN NUBIAN

Territory Types: Desert, Agricultural

Troop name		Troop Type				Capabilities		Points per base	Bases per BG	Total bases
C–in–C		Inspired Commander/Field Commander/Troop Commander						80/50/35	1	
Sub–commanders		Field Commander						50	0–2	
		Troop Commander						35	0–3	
		Type	Armour	Quality	Training	Shooting	Close Combat			
Core Troops										
Nubian cavalry		Light Horse	Unprotected	Average	Undrilled	Javelins	Light Spear	7	4–6	12–36
		Cavalry	Unprotected	Average	Undrilled	–	Light Spear, Swordsmen	8	4–6	
			Protected					9		6–18
Nubian and Beja camel riders		Camelry	Protected	Average	Undrilled	–	Light Spear	9	4–6	0–24
				Poor				7		
Archers		Medium Foot	Unprotected	Superior	Undrilled	Bow	–	6	6–8	16–96
				Average				5		
		Light Foot	Unprotected	Average	Undrilled	Bow	–	5	6–8	
Spearmen		Medium Foot	Protected	Poor	Undrilled	–	Defensive Spearmen	4	6–8	12–36
Optional Troops										
Noble cavalry		Cavalry	Armoured	Superior	Undrilled	–	Lancers, Swordsmen	16	4–6	0–6
Javelinmen		Light Foot	Unprotected	Poor	Undrilled	Javelins	Light Spear	2	6–8	0–8
Bedouin infantry	Only from 1175	Medium Foot	Protected	Average	Undrilled	–	Light Spear, Swordsmen	6	6–8	0–12
Bedouin cavalry		Light Horse	Unprotected	Average	Undrilled	–	Lancers, Swordsmen	8	4–6	0–12
		Cavalry	Unprotected	Average	Undrilled	–	Lancers, Swordsmen	8	4–6	
			Protected					9		
Allies										
Mamluk allies (Only from 1276) – See Field of Glory Companion 4: Swords and Scimitars: The Crusades										

AVAR

Arriving in Europe in the mid-6th century AD, the nomadic Avars rapidly subjugated the Kutrigur Huns (Bulgars) and the various Slavic tribes. Having been bought off by the Byzantine Emperor Justinian I, they invaded Germany and reached as far north as the Baltic before being fought to a standstill by the Franks. They then turned their attention to the Pannonian plain (modern Hungary), allying with the Lombards against the Gepids, who were subjugated in 567. Pressure on the Lombards then caused them to migrate into Italy in 568.

The Avars took to raiding the Balkan provinces of the Byzantine Empire. The Emperor Maurikios was campaigning against them beyond the Danube when his refusal to withdraw for the winter caused the army to mutiny. His subsequent

Avar Heavy Cavalry

murder provided the pretext for Sassanid Persian invasion, which gave the Avars a free hand in the Balkans. In 626, the Avars and Persians besieged Constantinople from each side of the Bosporus, but failed to capture it. The Avars then retreated to Pannonia, leaving their former Slav subjects in control of most of the former modern Yugoslavia, the interior of central Greece and much of the Peloponnese. The Bulgars threw off Avar control c.631.

At the beginning of the 9th century the Avar state was finally destroyed by the Franks under Charlemagne and the Bulgars under Krum. This list covers the Avars from 553 to 826.

TROOP NOTES

Although most Avar cavalry carried lance as well as bow, it is clear from the *Strategikon* that they were primarily horse archers, preferring to fight at a distance, so they do not have a Lancers POA. Bulgar heavy cavalry were charging lancers by the early 9th century at the latest – whether they fought in this way earlier or were more influenced by Avar tactical methods is uncertain.

AVAR STARTER ARMY		
Commander–in–Chief	1	Field Commander
Sub–commanders	2	2 x Troop Commander
Avar heavy cavalry	3 BGs	Each comprising 4 bases of Avar heavy cavalry: Superior, Armoured, Drilled Cavalry – Bow, Swordsmen
Bulgar heavy cavalry	1 BG	4 bases of Bulgar heavy cavalry: Superior, Armoured, Undrilled Cavalry – Bow, Swordsmen
Bulgar light cavalry	3 BGs	Each comprising 4 bases of Bulgar light cavalry: Average, Unprotected, Undrilled Light Horse – Bow, Swordsmen
Slav javelinmen	1 BG	6 bases of Slav javelinmen: Average, Protected, Undrilled Medium Foot – Light Spear
Slav archers	1 BG	6 bases of Slav archers: Average, Unprotected, Undrilled Light Foot – Bow
Camp	1	Unfortified camp
Total	9 BGs	Camp, 28 mounted bases, 12 foot bases, 3 commanders

BUILDING A CUSTOMISED LIST USING OUR ARMY POINTS

Choose an army based on the maxima and minima in the list below. The following special instructions apply to this army:

- Commanders should be depicted as Avar heavy cavalry.

AVAR									
Territory Types: Steppe, Agricultural (only from 558 to 631)									
C–in–C	Inspired Commander/Field Commander/Troop Commander						80/50/35	1	
Sub–commanders	Field Commander						50	0–2	
	Troop Commander						35	0–3	
Troop name	Troop Type				Capabilities		Points per base	Bases per BG	Total bases
	Type	Armour	Quality	Training	Shooting	Close Combat			
Core Troops									
Avar heavy cavalry	Cavalry	Armoured	Superior	Drilled	Bow	Swordsmen	19	4–6	8–48
Avar light cavalry	Light Horse	Unprotected	Average	Drilled	Bow	Swordsmen	10	4–6	0–12
	Cavalry	Unprotected	Average	Drilled	Bow	Swordsmen	10		
		Protected					11		
Bulgar heavy cavalry	Only from 558 to 631	Cavalry	Armoured	Superior	Undrilled	–	Lancers, Swordsmen	16	4–6	0–6
			Protected					12		
		Cavalry	Armoured	Superior	Undrilled	Bow	Swordsmen	18	4–6	
			Protected					14		
Bulgar light cavalry		Light Horse	Unprotected	Average	Undrilled	Bow	Swordsmen	10	4–6	6–24
		Cavalry	Unprotected	Average	Undrilled	Bow	Swordsmen	10		
			Protected					11		
Slav javelinmen		Medium Foot	Protected	Average	Undrilled	–	Light Spear	5	6–8	6–32
			Protected	Poor				3	6–8	
			Unprotected	Poor				2	8–12	
Slav archers		Light Foot	Unprotected	Average	Undrilled	Bow	–	5	6–8	0–8
				Poor				3		
Optional Troops									
Gepids	Cavalry	Armoured	Superior	Undrilled	–	Lancers, Swordsmen	16	4–6	0–8
		Protected					12		
Fortified camp							24		0–1
Allies									
Bulgar allies – Early Bulgar (Only from 675)									
Special campaigns									
Only in 626									
Sassanid allies – See Field of Glory Companion 5: *Legions Triumphant: Imperial Rome at War*									

AVAR ALLIES								
Allied commander		Field Commander/Troop Commander				40/25		1
Troop name		Troop Type				Capabilities		Points per base	Bases per BG	Total bases
		Type	Armour	Quality	Training	Shooting	Close Combat			
Avar heavy cavalry		Cavalry	Armoured	Superior	Drilled	Bow	Swordsmen	19	4–6	4–12
Avar light cavalry		Light Horse	Unprotected	Average	Drilled	Bow	Swordsmen	10	4	0–4
		Cavalry	Unprotected	Average	Drilled	Bow	Swordsmen	10		
			Protected					11		
Bulgar light cavalry	Only from 558 to 631	Light Horse	Unprotected	Average	Undrilled	Bow	Swordsmen	10	4–6	0–8
		Cavalry	Unprotected	Average	Undrilled	Bow	Swordsmen	10		
			Protected					11		
Slav javelinmen		Medium Foot	Protected	Average	Undrilled	–	Light Spear	5	6–8	0–12
			Protected	Poor				3	6–8	
			Unprotected	Poor				2	8–12	

WESTERN TURKISH

This list covers the Western Turks from the first appearance of the Göktürks around the mid-6th century until the final destruction of the Khazar Khaganate in the 11th century. The list also covers other Turkish tribes such as the Qarluqs, pre-Seljuq Oghuzz, and Turgesh.

Of all the groups covered by this list the Khazars lasted the longest and had the widest impact. Initially they were subject to the Göktürks but by the middle of the 7th century were fully independent. Their empire was based on the Volga river basin and stood astride a number of important trade routes from which they drew their wealth and much of their power. In addition to Turks the Khazars ruled Eastern Slavs and Alans amongst their subject populations. The Khaganate was decisively defeated

Khazar Commander

c.968 by the Kiev Rus led by Sviatoslav, who sacked the Khazar capital of Atil. There is some evidence that a remnant Khazar state continued to exist in the North Caucasus into the 11th century.

The Khazars are possibly most famous for their conversion to Judaism, around the middle of the 8th century. The story goes that the Khagan (Khazar ruler) asked a Muslim scholar which was better, Judaism or Christianity, to which he said the former. The Khagan then asked a Christian priest which was better, Judaism or Islam, and again received the answer Judaism. As both had said Judaism that is what he chose for his people. A theory that the Khazars were the ancestors of most modern East European Jews has not been supported by recent genetic studies.

TROOP NOTES

Although of Turkish descent, the Khazars are noted, and depicted, as using lances rather than being mainly horse archers. It is not clear when any change took place but it appears to have been by the mid-7th century. The Khazars trained by Herakeios in 627 may have influenced this change.

Khazar nobles are always depicted as heavily armoured. Grave finds show what appear to be dismounted noble cavalrymen fighting on foot with their lances held in both hands.

At some time in the 8th century, possibly following their defeat by the Arabs in 737, the Khazars recruited a standing army based around *Arsiyah* who were armoured horse archers rather like the later Abbasid *ghilman*. These were recruited from Muslims, mainly from Khwarism, on condition that they did not have to fight other Muslims. There may have been as many as 15,000 of these at their peak. We assume that these would not be available to a remnant Khazar state after 968.

Many Khazar subjects fought in a similar manner to their overlords so are not shown separately.

BUILDING A CUSTOMISED LIST USING OUR ARMY POINTS

Choose an army based on the maxima and minima in the list below. The following special instructions apply to this army:

- Commanders should be depicted as noble cavalry.
- From 627 all noble cavalry in a Khazar army or allied contingent must be Lancers. Before that they can be either all Bowmen or all Lancers.
- Khazar noble cavalry can always dismount as Heavy Foot, Armoured, Superior, Undrilled, Offensive Spearmen.
- The minimum marked * is reduced to 4 for Khazar armies between 738 and 968.

WESTERN TURKISH

Territory Types: Steppe, Agricultural

C–in–C		Inspired Commander/Field Commander/Troop Commander						80/50/35	1	
Sub–commanders		Field Commander						50	0–2	
		Troop Commander						35	0–3	
Troop name		Troop Type				Capabilities		Points per base	Bases per BG	Total bases
		Type	Armour	Quality	Training	Shooting	Close Combat			
Core Troops										
Noble cavalry	Any	Cavalry	Armoured	Superior	Undrilled	Bow	Swordsmen	18	4–6	4–24
			Protected					14		
	Only Khazars	Cavalry	Armoured	Superior	Undrilled	–	Lancers, Swordsmen	16		
Arsiyah	Only Khazars from 738 to 968	Cavalry	Armoured	Superior	Drilled	Bow	Swordsmen	19	4–6	8–24
Other horse archers		Light Horse	Unprotected	Average	Undrilled	Bow	Swordsman	10	4–6	*12–64
		Cavalry	Unprotected	Average	Undrilled	Bow	Swordsmen	10		
			Protected					11		
Slav javelinmen	Only Khazars from 651 to 968	Medium Foot	Protected	Average	Undrilled	–	Light Spear	5	6–8	0–24
			Protected	Poor				3	6–8	
			Unprotected	Poor				2	8–12	
Slav archers		Light Foot	Unprotected	Average	Undrilled	Bow	–	5	6–8	0–12
				Poor				3		
Slav skirmishing javelinmen		Light Foot	Unprotected	Average	Undrilled	Javelins	Light Spear	4	6–8	
				Poor				2		

Optional Troops									
Fortified camp							24		0–1
Guard infantry	Only Khazars before 969	Heavy Foot	Armoured	Average	Undrilled	–	Defensive Spearmen	8	6–8	0–8
Artillery		Heavy Artillery	–	Average	–	Heavy Artillery	–	20	2	0–2
Foot archers		Medium Foot	Unprotected	Poor	Undrilled	Bow	–	3	6–8	0–12
		Light Foot	Unprotected	Poor	Undrilled	Bow	–	3		
Khazar city militia or Turkish levy		Mob	Unprotected	Poor	Undrilled	–	–	2	8–12	0–12
Allies									
Utigur allies (Only Göktürks in 576) – Early Bulgar									
Sogdian allies (Only Turgesh) – Central Asian City States – See Note p.78									
Tibetan allies (Only Turgesh) – See Note p.78									
Oghuzz allies (Only Khazars from 780) – Western Turkish									

WESTERN TURKISH ALLIES

Allied commander		Field Commander/Troop Commander						40/25		1	
Troop name		Troop Type				Capabilities		Points per base	Bases per BG	Total bases
		Type	Armour	Quality	Training	Shooting	Close Combat			
Core Troops										
Noble cavalry	Any	Cavalry	Armoured	Superior	Undrilled	Bow	Swordsmen	18	4–6	0–8
			Protected					14		
	Only Khazars	Cavalry	Armoured	Superior	Undrilled	–	Lancers, Swordsmen	16		
Other horse archers		Light Horse	Unprotected	Average	Undrilled	Bow	Swordsmen	10	4–6	4–18
		Cavalry	Unprotected	Average	Undrilled	Bow	Swordsmen	10		
			Protected					11		

ARAB CONQUEST

This list covers Islamic Arab armies from c.629 AD. Although armies had existed before that time they only numbered a few hundred men. The list ends c.685 when the fifth Umayyad caliph, 'Abd al-Malik, changed the Muslim army from being tribally based to a "regular" structure.

Arab armies of the conquest period hardly differed from those of the pre-Islamic period in equipment, organisation or tactics, however the new Muslim faith gave them greater discipline and cohesion as well as a motivation based on the ideology of Islam. The benefit of this cohesion is demonstrated by the victories of Arab armies over numerically larger Roman and

Camel Mounted Scout and Skirmishers

Soldiers of the Great Expansion, by Angus McBride. Taken from Men-at-Arms 255: Armies of the Muslim Conquest.

Persian forces, such as at the battles of Yarmuk and Qadisiyya in 636, and Nihawand in 642.

The biggest challenge to the Muslim state followed the death of the Prophet in 632 when large numbers of tribes either seceded from the state or renounced Islam entirely; some even followed a false prophet called Musaylimah ibn Habib. A short but decisive series of wars, known as the Ridda Wars, ensued, returning the Arabian peninsular to Muslim control.

Non-Muslims faced by an Arab army would traditionally be offered three alternatives – to convert to Islam with the same rights and responsibilities as any other Muslim, to remain in their current religion but pay a higher rate of tax, or war to the finish. The offer often stated that in the case of the latter the Muslims loved death more than their enemies loved life as the Muslim who died was guaranteed a place in paradise.

KHALID IBN AL-WALID

Whilst undoubtedly one of the greatest Arab generals of the conquest period, he is hardly known. Initially opposed to Mohammed, he fought in the Meccan army sent to destroy the fledgling Muslim state. In 625, at the Battle of Uhud, Khalid led the Meccan cavalry in a charge that turned the battle and caused many casualties amongst the Muslims, with even the Prophet being slightly wounded. However, in 628, Khalid converted to Islam and thereafter fought in many of the wars of conquest.

Khalid commanded the army sent to invade Persian Iraq, which he conquered in just over a year, and was subsequently sent to Syria to do the same against the Byzantines. Khalid's greatest achievement is often said to be his transfer of hundreds of soldiers from the Iraq front to Syria across the desert, a march many felt was impossible. He achieved this by using camels as living water containers, slaughtering them during the march across the waterless desert in order to sustain the horses of his force whilst the men drank the camels' blood. Khalid also once managed to defeat the Persians with a numerically inferior force using a form of the double envelopment strategy – only previously successfully used by an army smaller than that of its opponents by Hannibal at Cannae.

The second caliph, 'Umar, who had always disliked Khalid, dismissed him from command of the army, though he remained in charge of the cavalry. His actions at the Battle of Yarmuk against the Byzantines were decisive and led to the Arab victory and the conquest of Syria.

Khalid continued to fight in Syria until 638. He died in 642 having fought, it is claimed, over 100 battles and having never been defeated.

TROOP NOTES

Until c.638, Muslim armies relied mainly on their infantry. With the acquisition of large numbers of horses in 638, many of the foot warriors were upgraded to cavalry in the new standing Jund forces settled in permanent camps in the conquered areas. Average grading reflects their initial inexperience in mounted fighting.

Whilst swords played an important part in Arab fighting, classifying the infantry warriors as Offensive Spearmen gives the correct results and emphasises the cohesion demonstrated by their armies.

Following the conquest of Persia, a number of Sassanid troops joined the Arab army but continued to fight in their normal manner. Dailami represent the former guard of the Sassanid governor of Iraq who also joined the Arabs.

ARAB CONQUEST STARTER ARMY		
Commander-in-Chief	1	Field Commander
Sub-commanders	2	2 x Troop Commander
Jund cavalry	2 BGs	Each comprising 6 bases of Jund cavalry: Average, Protected, Undrilled Cavalry – Lancers, Swordsmen
Persian cavalry	1 BG	4 bases of Persian cavalry: Superior, Armoured, Undrilled Cavalry – Bow, Swordsmen
Bedouin cavalry	2 BGs	Each comprising 4 bases of Bedouin cavalry: Average, Unprotected, Undrilled Light Horse – Lancers, Swordsmen
Foot warriors	2 BGs	Each comprising 8 bases of foot warriors: Superior, Protected, Undrilled Heavy Foot – Offensive Spearmen
Archers	2 BGs	Each comprising 6 bases of archers: Superior, Unprotected, Undrilled Light Foot – Bow
Slingers	1 BG	4 bases of slingers: Superior, Unprotected, Undrilled Light Foot – Sling
Camp	1	Unfortified camp
Total	10 BGs	Camp, 24 mounted bases, 32 foot bases, 3 commanders

BUILDING A CUSTOMISED LIST USING OUR ARMY POINTS

Choose an army based on the maxima and minima in the list below. The following special instructions apply to this army:

- Commanders should be depicted as foot warriors or Jund cavalry.
- Jund cavalry can always dismount as Heavy Foot, Superior, Undrilled, Protected, - , Offensive Spearmen.

ARAB CONQUEST

Territory Types: Desert (only before 638), Agricultural, Developed (only from 638)

Troop name		Type	Armour	Quality	Training	Shooting	Close Combat	Points per base	Bases per BG	Total bases
C–in–C		Inspired Commander/Field Commander/Troop Commander						80/50/35		1
Sub–commanders		Field Commander						50		0–2
		Troop Commander						35		0–3
Troop name		Troop Type				Capabilities		Points per base	Bases per BG	Total bases
		Type	Armour	Quality	Training	Shooting	Close Combat			
Core Troops										
Foot warriors	Before 638	Heavy Foot	Protected	Superior	Undrilled	–	Offensive Spearmen	9	2/3 or all	24–84
	From 638								8–9	12–48
Supporting archers		Light Foot	Unprotected	Superior	Undrilled	Bow	–	6	1/3 or 0	0–24
Separately deployed archers		Medium Foot	Protected	Superior	Undrilled	Bow	–	8	6–8	0–24
				Average				6		0–12
		Light Foot	Unprotected	Superior	Undrilled	Bow	–	6	6–8	
				Average				5		
Jund cavalry	Only from 638	Cavalry	Protected	Superior	Undrilled	–	Lancers, Swordsmen	12	4–6	12–24
				Average				9		
Optional Troops										
City cavalry		Cavalry	Armoured	Superior	Undrilled	–	Lancers, Swordsmen	16	4–6	0–6
			Armoured	Average				12		
			Protected	Superior				12		
			Protected	Average				9		
Bedouin cavalry		Light Horse	Unprotected	Superior	Undrilled	–	Lancers, Swordsmen	10	4–6	0–12
				Average				8		
		Cavalry	Unprotected	Superior	Undrilled	–	Lancers, Swordsmen	10	4–6	
			Unprotected	Average				8		
			Protected	Superior				12		
			Protected	Average				9		
Camel-mounted scouts		Camelry	Unprotected	Superior	Undrilled	Bow	–	12	4	0–4
				Average				10		
Persian cavalry	Only from 638	Cavalry	Armoured	Superior	Undrilled	Bow	Swordsmen	18	4	0–4
Slingers		Light Foot	Unprotected	Superior	Undrilled	Sling	–	5	4–6	0–6
				Average				4		
Javelinmen		Medium Foot	Protected	Superior	Undrilled	–	Light Spear	7	6–8	0–8
				Average				5		
		Light Foot	Unprotected	Superior	Undrilled	Javelins	Light Spear	5	6–8	
				Average				4		
Dailami	Only from 636	Medium Foot	Protected	Superior	Drilled	–	Impact foot, Swordsmen	10	2/3 or all	0–6
			Armoured					13	6	
		Light Foot	Unprotected	Superior	Drilled	Bow	–	6	1/3 or 0	
Fortified camp								24		0–1
Special Campaigns										
Only in 636										
Disguised camels		Camelry	Protected	Poor	Undrilled	–	–	6	4	0–4

EARLY BULGAR

The Bulgars were initially a coalition of Hunnic tribes (Kutrigurs and Utigurs). This list covers Bulgar armies of the Khanate of Greater Bulgaria (around the Sea of Azov) from 631, when they threw off Avar rule, until their defeat by the Khazars c.668, after which part of the horde fled north and part fled west. The western branch, under Khan Asparukh, formed the Danubian Bulgar kingdom c.680, incorporating the local Slavic tribes. This list covers that kingdom until its conquest by the Byzantines in 1018. The northern branch fled up the Volga and formed the Volga Bulgar state, which is not covered by this list. Khan Krum (803–814) conquered large chunks of Byzantine territory and advanced to the walls of Constantinople, but died before he could press the assault.

In the Danubian Bulgar state, the Bulgars initially remained a separate elite, but by the reign of Boris I (852–889), who accepted Christianity in 864, the distinctions had become blurred. "Bulgarian" foot could be Slav, Bulgar, Vlach or Greek.

Byzantine allies represent the Greek *Themes* who went over to Krum and his successors – they fought loyally under their own generals. When the Bulgars were forced to hand back the Byzantine provinces, these Thematic troops were transferred to other parts of Bulgaria where they continued to serve. Presumably they eventually lost their distinctive character.

Wooden palisades were sometimes used to block off whole valleys.

TROOP NOTES

Bulgar boyars were charging lancers by the early 9th century at the latest – whether they fought in this way earlier or were more influenced by Avar tactical methods is uncertain.

Boyar Cavalry

EARLY BULGAR STARTER ARMY		
Commander-in-Chief	1	Troop Commander
Sub-commanders	2	2 x Troop Commander
Boyars	2 BGs	Each comprising 4 bases of boyars: Superior, Armoured, Undrilled Cavalry – Lancers, Swordsmen
Boyars	2 BGs	Each comprising 4 bases of boyars: Superior, Protected, Undrilled Cavalry – Lancers, Swordsmen
Bulgar horse archers	3 BGs	Each comprising 4 bases of Bulgar horse archers: Average, Unprotected, Undrilled Light Horse – Bow, Swordsmen
Bulgarian spearmen	2 BGs	Each comprising 8 bases of Bulgarian spearmen: Average, Protected, Undrilled Heavy Foot – Defensive Spearmen
Bulgarian archers	1 BG	8 bases of Bulgarian archers: Average, Unprotected, Undrilled Light Foot – Bow
Camp	1	Unfortified camp
Total	10 BGs	Camp, 28 mounted bases, 24 foot bases, 3 commanders

BUILDING A CUSTOMISED LIST USING OUR ARMY POINTS

Choose an army based on the maxima and minima in the list below. The following special instructions apply to this army:

- Commanders should be depicted as boyars.
- Before 803, boyars can have either lancers or bow capability, but all must have the same.
- The minima marked * only apply if any foot are used.

EARLY BULGAR

Territory Types: Steppe, Agricultural (only from 680), Hilly (only from 680), Woodlands (only from 680)

Troop name		Troop Type				Capabilities		Points per base	Bases per BG	Total bases
C–in–C		Inspired Commander/Field Commander/Troop Commander						80/50/35	1	
Sub–commanders		Field Commander						50	0–2	
		Troop Commander						35	0–3	
		Type	Armour	Quality	Training	Shooting	Close Combat			
Core Troops										
Boyars	Only before 803	Cavalry	Armoured	Superior	Undrilled	Bow	Swordsmen	18	4–6	4–24
			Protected					14		
	Any date	Cavalry	Armoured	Superior	Undrilled	–	Lancers, Swordsmen	16		
			Protected					12		
Bulgar horse archers		Light Horse	Unprotected	Average	Undrilled	Bow	Swordsmen	10	4–6	16–72 before 680, 8–30 from 680
		Cavalry	Unprotected	Average	Undrilled	Bow	Swordsmen	10		
			Protected					11		
Slav cavalry		Cavalry	Protected	Superior	Undrilled	–	Light Spear, Swordsmen	12	4–6	0–6
			Armoured					16		
Slav javelinmen	Only from 680 to 851	Medium Foot	Protected	Average	Undrilled	–	Light Spear	5	6–8	12–64
			Protected	Poor				3	6–8	
			Unprotected	Poor				2	8–12	
Slav archers		Light Foot	Unprotected	Average	Undrilled	Bow	–	5	6–8	0–12
				Poor				3		
Slav skirmishing javelinmen		Light Foot	Unprotected	Average	Undrilled	Javelins	Light Spear	4	6–8	0–8
				Poor				2		
Bulgarian spearmen	Only from 852	Heavy Foot	Protected	Average	Undrilled	–	Defensive Spearmen	6	6–8	12–48
				Poor				4		
Bulgarian archers		Medium Foot	Unprotected	Average	Undrilled	Bow	–	5	6–8	0–24
				Poor				3		
		Light Foot	Unprotected	Average	Undrilled	Bow	–	5	6–8	
				Poor				3		
Optional Troops										
Fortified camp	Only before 680							24		0–1
Field defences	Only from 680	Field Fortifications						3		0–24
"Civilised Slavs" or Greek militia	Only from 803	Heavy Foot	Protected	Average	Undrilled	–	Defensive Spearmen	6	6–8	0–12
				Poor				4	6–8	
		Heavy Foot	Protected	Poor	Drilled	–	Defensive Spearmen	5	6–8	
Allies										
Avar allies (Only in 812)										
Byzantine allies – Thematic Byzantine (803 to 852)										
Pecheneg allies (Only in 896)										

EARLY BULGAR ALLIES

Allied Commander	Field Commander/Troop Commander						40/25	1	
Troop name	**Troop Type**				**Capabilities**		**Points per base**	**Bases per BG**	**Total bases**
	Type	Armour	Quality	Training	Shooting	Close Combat			
Boyars	Only before 803	Cavalry	Armoured	Superior	Undrilled	Bow	Swordsmen	18	4–6	4–8
			Protected					14		
	Any date	Cavalry	Armoured	Superior	Undrilled	–	Lancers, Swordsmen	16		
			Protected					12		
Bulgar horse archers		Light Horse	Unprotected	Average	Undrilled	Bow	Swordsmen	10	4–6	4–12
		Cavalry	Unprotected	Average	Undrilled	Bow	Swordsmen	10		
			Protected					11		
Slav javelinmen	Only from 680 to 851	Medium Foot	Protected	Average	Undrilled	–	Light Spear	5	6–8	*6–18
			Protected	Poor				3	6–8	
			Unprotected	Poor				2	8–12	
Slav archers		Light Foot	Unprotected	Average	Undrilled	Bow	–	5	4–6	0–6
				Poor				3		
Bulgarian spearmen		Heavy Foot	Protected	Average	Undrilled	–	Defensive Spearmen	6	6–8	*6–16
				Poor				4		
Bulgarian archers	Only from 852	Medium Foot	Unprotected	Average	Undrilled	Bow	–	5	6–8	0–8
				Poor				3		
		Light Foot	Unprotected	Average	Undrilled	Bow	–	5	6–8	
				Poor				3		

THEMATIC BYZANTINE

The Thematic system was initiated by the Emperor Herakleios (610–641) in response to the dangers besetting the Byzantine Empire in the first half of the 7th century. The Empire was divided into a number of administrative areas termed themes. The soldiers in each theme were granted plots of land to farm, in return for part-time military service. They did not own their land, which was still owned by the state, but pay requirements were correspondingly reduced. Moreover, their descendants would be expected to follow them as thematic soldiers, removing the need for unpopular conscription from the general population. The commander of each theme adopted the dual role of military commander and civil governor – thus reversing the division between civil and military government instituted by Diocletian in the 3rd century. The Thematic system gave the Empire a new resilience that allowed it to prosper for centuries.

This list covers Byzantine armies from the completion of the Thematic system c.650 until the accession of Nikephoros II Phokas in 963.

TROOP NOTES

Thematic troops were locally based part-timers, supplying their own equipment, and were divided into first-class and second-class. It was considered preferable to summon reinforcements from another theme rather than use one's own second-class troops. Thematic cavalry generally fought

Byzantine Commander

Skoutatos

10 ranks deep. The rear rank archers are treated as the same armour class as the lancers, even though they probably usually had less armour. When detached, however, they are graded according to their own true armour class.

Centrally-based professional Tagmatic units were introduced c.740. They are graded as Bow* because only 2 out of their 5 ranks were armed with bows.

The *kataphraktoi* formed in a deep wedge, designed to break into the enemy army.

The 14,000 Khurramite sectarians who went over to the Byzantines in the second quarter of the 9th century, and who were later joined by 16,000 more deserters from the formerly Christian provinces of the Caliphate, fought in their own units. They were probably later assimilated into normal Byzantine units, but we assume that initially at least they would have retained their previous fighting style.

BLACK SEA

Serbs

Bulgar Khanate

MEDITERRANEAN SEA

N

The empire c.750
Territory reconquered by c.920
Lost to Lombards or local princes c.751
Lost to Saracens c.820–930

0   250 miles
0   500 km

1. Exarchate of Ravenna.
2. Venetia and Istria.
3. Duchy of Rome.
4. Duchy of Naples.
5. Duchy of Calabria.
6. Thema of Hellas.
7. Thema of Thrace.
8. Thema of Opsikion.
9. Thema of Thrakesion.
10. Thema of Anatolikon.
11. Thema of Kibyrrhaiotai.
12. Thema of Armeniakon.

The Byzantine Empire c. AD 700–950. Taken from Essential Histories 33: Byzantium at War.

THEMATIC BYZANTINE STARTER ARMY		
Commander-in-Chief	1	Field Commander
Sub-commanders	2	2 x Troop Commander
Thematic cavalry	4 BGs	Each comprising 4 bases of Thematic cavalry: Average, Armoured, Drilled Cavalry – 2 Lancers, Swordsmen, 2 Bow, Swordsmen
Detached Koursores	2 BGs	Each comprising 4 bases of Koursores: Average, Protected, Drilled Cavalry – Bow, Swordsmen
Alan mercenaries	1 BG	4 bases of Alan mercenaries: Average, Unprotected, Undrilled Light Horse – Bow, Swordsmen
Skoutatoi and attached archers	2 BGs	Each comprising 8 bases of skoutatoi and attached archers: 6 Poor, Protected, Drilled Heavy Foot – Defensive Spearmen, 2 Poor, Unprotected, Drilled Light Foot - Bow
Archers in separate units	1 BG	8 bases of archers: Average, Unprotected, Drilled Light Foot – Bow
Slingers	1 BG	4 bases of slingers: Poor, Unprotected, Drilled Light Foot – Sling
Camp	1	Unfortified camp
Total	11 BGs	Camp, 28 mounted bases, 28 foot bases, 3 commanders

BUILDING A CUSTOMISED LIST USING OUR ARMY POINTS

Choose an army based on the maxima and minima in the list below. The following special instructions apply to this army:

- Commanders should be depicted as first class Thematic or Tagmatic cavalry.
- *Kataphraktoi* bowmen shoot as if cavalry.
- Only one allied contingent can be used.
- Georgians, Bulgars or Alans cannot be used with Moors.

THEMATIC BYZANTINE										
Territory Types: Agricultural, Developed, Hilly, Mountains										
C–in–C		Inspired Commander/Field Commander/Troop Commander						80/50/35	1	
Sub–commanders		Field Commander						50	0–2	
		Troop Commander						35	0–3	
Troop name		Troop Type				Capabilities		Points per base	Bases per BG	Total bases
		Type	Armour	Quality	Training	Shooting	Close Combat			
Core Troops										
Tagmatic cavalry	Only from 740	Cavalry	Armoured	Superior	Drilled	Bow*	Lancers, Swordsmen	19	4–6	0–12
First class Thematic cavalry		Cavalry	Armoured	Average	Drilled	–	Lancers, Swordsmen	13	1/2 4–6	12–36
		Cavalry	Armoured	Average	Drilled	Bow	Swordsmen	15	1/2	
Second class Thematic cavalry		Cavalry	Protected	Poor	Drilled	–	Lancers, Swordsmen	8	1/2 4–6	0–12
		Cavalry	Protected	Poor	Drilled	Bow	Swordsmen	10	1/2	
Detached Koursores		Cavalry	Armoured	Superior	Drilled	Bow	Swordsmen	19	4–6	0–1 per 2 Tagmatic cavalry
		Cavalry	Protected	Average	Drilled	Bow	Swordsmen	12	4–6	0–1 per 2 1st class Thematic cavalry
		Cavalry	Unprotected	Poor	Drilled	Bow	Swordsmen	9	4–6	0–1 per 2 2nd class Thematic cavalry

Skoutatoi and attached archers		Heavy Foot	Protected	Average	Drilled	—	Defensive Spearmen	7	3/4	8–12	0–16
		Light Foot	Unprotected	Average	Drilled	Bow	—	5	1/4		
		Heavy Foot	Protected	Poor	Drilled	—	Defensive Spearmen	5	3/4	8–12	
		Light Foot	Unprotected	Poor	Drilled	Bow	—	3	1/4		
Archers in separate units		Medium Foot	Unprotected	Average	Drilled	Bow	—	6		6–8	0–8
				Poor				4			
		Light Foot	Unprotected	Average	Drilled	Bow	—	5		6–8	
				Poor				3			
Optional Troops											
Kataphraktoi	Only from 904	Cataphracts	Heavily Armoured	Elite	Drilled	—	Lancers, Swordsmen	23	1/2	2	0–2
		Cataphracts	Heavily Armoured	Elite	Drilled	Bow	Swordsmen	25	1/2		
		Cataphracts	Heavily Armoured	Superior	Drilled	—	Lancers, Swordsmen	20	1/2	2	
		Cataphracts	Heavily Armoured	Superior	Drilled	Bow	Swordsmen	22	1/2		
Menavlatoi	Only from 904	Heavy Foot	Protected	Average	Drilled	—	Heavy Weapon	8	4	0–4	
Javelinmen		Light Foot	Unprotected	Average	Drilled	Javelins	Light Spear	4	4	0–4	
				Poor				2			
Slingers		Light Foot	Unprotected	Average	Drilled	Sling	—	4	4	0–4	
				Poor				2			
Georgian cavalry		Cavalry	Armoured	Superior	Undrilled	—	Lancers, Swordsmen	16	4	0–4	
Bulgar or Alan mercenaries		Light Horse	Unprotected	Average	Undrilled	Bow	Swordsmen	10			
		Cavalry	Unprotected	Average	Undrilled	Bow	Swordsmen	10	4	0–4	
			Protected					11			
Khurramite and other deserters from the Caliphate	Only from 834 to 839	Cavalry	Armoured	Average	Undrilled	—	Lancers, Swordsmen	12	4–6	0–12	
Bolt–shooters		Heavy Artillery	–	Average	–	Heavy Artillery	–	20	2	0–2	
Fortified Camp								24		0–1	
Allies											
Slav allies – Early South Slav											
Moorish allies – Later Moorish (Only in 681)											

Byzantine abbot and retinue, by Angus McBride. Taken from Men-at-Arms 247: Romano-Byzantine Armies 4th–9th Centuries.

THEMATIC BYZANTINE ALLIES										
Allied commander		Field Commander/Troop Commander					40/25		1	
Troop name		Troop Type				Capabilities		Points per base	Bases per BG	Total bases
		Type	Armour	Quality	Training	Shooting	Close Combat			
Tagmatic cavalry	Only after 740	Cavalry	Armoured	Superior	Drilled	Bow*	Lancers, Swordsmen	19	4	0–4
Thematic cavalry		Cavalry	Armoured	Average	Drilled	–	Lancers, Swordsmen	13	1/2 4–6	4–12
		Cavalry	Armoured	Average	Drilled	Bow	Swordsmen	15	1/2	
Detached Koursores		Cavalry	Protected	Average	Drilled	Bow	Swordsmen	12	4–6	0–1 per 2 Tagmatic and Thematic cavalry
Skoutatoi and attached archers		Heavy Foot	Protected	Average	Drilled	–	Defensive Spearmen	7	3/4 8	0–8
		Light Foot	Unprotected	Average	Drilled	Bow	–	5	1/4	
		Heavy Foot	Protected	Poor	Drilled	–	Defensive Spearmen	5	3/4 8	0–8
		Light Foot	Unprotected	Poor	Drilled	Bow	–	3	1/4	
Archers in separate units		Medium Foot	Unprotected	Average	Drilled	Bow	–	6	4	0–4
				Poor				4		
		Light Foot	Unprotected	Average	Drilled	Bow	–	5	4	
				Poor				3		

UMAYYAD ARAB

This list covers the armies of the Arab caliphate from the development of a "regular" army c.685 AD until the victory of the Abbasids led by Abu Muslim over the Umayyads in 750 at the Battle of the Zab. It does not cover the later Umayyad state in Spain.

Although the Umayyads came to power in 661 there was no change to the Arab army until the reign of 'Abd al-Malik (685–705) who, as part of the continuing attempt to centralise the caliphate, reformed the army so that it was no longer tribal in basis. Troops remained broadly the same although increasing reliance was placed on cavalry with the infantry adopting a more defensive tactical role.

Despite continuing instability within the caliphate, the Umayyads maintained their wars of conquest. Visigothic Spain was invaded in 711 and even France was subject to raids in force until the Battle of Tours (Poitiers) in 732. In the east, Khurasan was finally secured with the defeat of the Turkish Khazars and Turgesh. The main military failure of the Umayyads was the abortive siege of Constantinople which lasted from 717 to 718.

Umayyad Foot

The Umayyads were also great builders and the Dome of the Rock mosque in Jerusalem was built under their patronage.

TROOP NOTES

The quality of the *Jund* troops outside of the Syrian Ahl al-Sham declined over time.

UMAYYAD ARAB STARTER ARMY		
Commander-in-Chief	1	Field Commander
Sub-commanders	2	2 x Troop Commander
Jund cavalry	3 BGs	Each comprising 4 bases of Jund cavalry: Superior, Armoured, Drilled Cavalry – Lancers, Swordsmen
Bedouin cavalry	1 BG	4 bases of Bedouin cavalry: Average, Unprotected, Undrilled Light Horse – Lancers, Swordsmen
Khurasanian light horse archers	1 BG	4 bases of Khurasanian light horse archers: Average, Unprotected, Undrilled Light Horse – Bow
Spearmen and archers	3 BGs	Each comprising 9 bases of spearmen and archers: 6 Average, Protected, Drilled Heavy Foot – Defensive Spearmen, 3 Average, Unprotected, Drilled Light Foot - Bow
Separately deployed archers	1 BG	8 bases of archers: Average, Unprotected, Drilled Light Foot – Bow
Camp	1	Unfortified camp
Total	9 BGs	Camp, 20 mounted bases, 35 foot bases, 3 commanders

Umayyad cavalry, by Angus McBride. Taken from Men-at-Arms 255: Armies of the Muslim Conquest.

BUILDING A CUSTOMISED LIST USING OUR ARMY POINTS

Choose an army based on the maxima and minima in the list below. The following special instructions apply to this army:

- Commanders should be depicted as *Jund* cavalry.
- *Jund* cavalry can always dismount as Heavy Foot, Superior, Average or Poor (as per mounted class), Drilled, Armoured, - , Defensive Spearmen.
- Berbers cannot be used with any other allies, nor with Khurasanians, Turks, Dailami or Hillmen.

Umayyad Archer

Umayyad infantry, by Angus McBride. Taken from *Men-at-Arms 255: Armies of the Muslim Conquest.*

Umayyad guardsmen, by Angus McBride. Taken from Men-at-Arms 125: The Armies of Islam
7th–11th Centuries.

UMAYYAD ARAB

Territory Types: Agricultural, Developed, Hilly, Mountains

C–in–C		Inspired Commander/Field Commander/Troop Commander				80/50/35		1	
Sub–commanders		Field Commander				50		0–2	
		Troop Commander				35		0–3	
Troop name	Troop Type				Capabilities		Points per base	Bases per BG	Total bases
	Type	Armour	Quality	Training	Shooting	Close Combat			
Core Troops									
Jund cavalry	Cavalry	Armoured	Superior	Drilled	–	Lancers, Swordsmen	17	4–6	6–32
			Average				13		
			Poor				10		
Spearmen and archers	Heavy Foot	Protected	Average	Drilled	–	Defensive Spearmen	7	2/3 9–12	18–48
	Light Foot	Unprotected	Average	Drilled	Bow	–	5	1/3	
	Heavy Foot	Protected	Poor	Drilled	–	Defensive Spearmen	5	2/3 9–12	
	Light Foot	Unprotected	Poor	Drilled	Bow	–	3	1/3	
Separately deployed archers	Medium Foot	Protected	Average	Drilled	Bow	–	7	6–8	0–8
			Poor				5		
	Light Foot	Unprotected	Average	Drilled	Bow	–	5	6–8	
			Poor				3		
Fortified camp							24		0–1
Optional Troops									
Ghazi cavalry	Light Horse	Unprotected	Superior	Undrilled	–	Lancers, Swordsmen	10	4–6	0–6
	Cavalry	Unprotected	Superior	Undrilled	–	Lancers, Swordsmen	10	4–6	
		Protected					12		
Bedouin cavalry	Light Horse	Unprotected	Average	Undrilled	–	Lancers, Swordsmen	8	4–6	0–6
	Cavalry	Unprotected	Average	Undrilled	–	Lancers, Swordsmen	8	4–6	
		Protected					9		
Khurasanian light horse archers	Light Horse	Unprotected	Average	Undrilled	Bow	–	8	4	0–4
Turkish cavalry	Light Horse	Unprotected	Average	Undrilled	Bow	Swordsmen	10	4	
	Cavalry	Unprotected	Average	Undrilled	Bow	Swordsmen	10		
		Protected					11		
Dailami	Medium Foot	Protected	Superior	Drilled	–	Impact foot, Swordsmen	10	2/3 or all 6–9	0–9
		Armoured					13		
	Light Foot	Unprotected	Superior	Drilled	Bow	–	6	1/3 or 0	
Hillmen	Medium Foot	Protected	Average	Undrilled	–	Light Spear	5	6–8	
	Light Foot	Unprotected	Average	Undrilled	Javelins	Light Spear	4	6–8	
	Light Foot	Unprotected	Average	Undrilled	Bow	–	5	6–8	
Berber light horse	Light Horse	Unprotected	Average	Undrilled	Javelins	Light Spear	7	4–6	0–12
Berber javelinmen	Light Foot	Unprotected	Average	Undrilled	Javelins	Light Spear	4	6–8	0–16
Bolt–shooters or stone–throwers	Heavy Artillery	–	Average	–	Heavy Artillery	–	20	2	0–2
Allies									
Khurasanian allies – Central Asian City States – See Note p.78									
Berber allies – Later Moorish									
Tibetan allies – See Note p.78									

ABBASID ARAB

This list covers armies of the Abbasid Caliphate from the initial Abbasid revolt in 747 AD until 946 when the Buwayhids captured Baghdad and the temporal power of the Caliphate ceased to exist.

Instability within the Umayyad caliphate eventually led to a revolution in favour of the caliph being a member of the family of the Prophet. Despite expectation that this would be a descendant of the fourth caliph, 'Ali, it turned out that the Khurasan based family of the Prophet's uncle, 'Abbas ibn Abd al-Muttalib seized power, ruling as the Abbasid dynasty. To bolster their revolt, the Abbasids adopted black flags to fulfil a prophecy that an army would come from the east under black banners.

Initial Abbasid armies were very similar to Umayyad ones, but in 794 a new army known as the Abbasiya was raised in Khurasan. This probably included traditional armoured horse archers. The biggest change to Muslim armies came in the wake of the civil war of 811–813 when the future caliph al-Mu'tasim started to recruit Turkish slaves into the army. These became the famous ghilman (ghulam) cavalry, soon coming to dominate the Abbasid military. Subsequently, they were the backbone of the armies of many of the Muslim successor states. Similar professional troops were raised from non-slave recruits in the East.

This list also covers the Tulunid and Ikhshidid Egyptian states created by Abbasid governors who assumed independence as Abbasid authority failed. The Tulunids ruled independently from 874 until 905 when the Abbasids regained control. The Ikhshidids ruled independently from 937 until 969 when they were conquered by the Fatimids. Their armies were based on Turkish ghilman and black slave troops.

TROOP NOTES

The armament of the black troops is uncertain. In Fatimid armies some were close order infantry fighting with javelins and swords. We allow both for this possibility and for the possibility that they fought as traditional style spearmen but merely supplied the manpower.

Abna' were the descendants of the original Abbasid army who settled in Baghdad. They fought as normal Arab cavalry and infantry and so are included in the Arab cavalry and spearmen and archers lines in this list.

Naffatun were armed with naphtha bombs – the medieval equivalent of Molotov cocktails.

Abbasid Troop Commander

Abbasid Spearman

Abbasid frontier soldiers, by Angus McBride. Taken from Men-at-Arms 255: Armies of the Muslim Conquest.

ABBASID ARAB STARTER ARMY		
Commander-in-Chief	1	Field Commander
Sub-commanders	2	2 x Troop Commander
Turkish ghilman	3 BGs	Each comprising 4 bases of Turkish ghilman: Superior, Armoured, Drilled Cavalry – Bow, Swordsmen
Bedouin cavalry	1 BG	4 bases of Bedouin cavalry: Average, Unprotected, Undrilled Light Horse – Lancers, Swordsmen
Black slave soldiers	3 BGs	Each comprising 9 bases of black slave soldiers: 6 Average, Protected, Drilled Heavy Foot – Defensive Spearmen, 3 Average, Unprotected, Drilled Light Foot – Bow
Separately deployed archers	1 BG	6 bases of archers: Average, Unprotected, Undrilled Light Foot – Bow
Naffatun	1 BG	4 bases of naffatun: Average, Unprotected, Undrilled Light Foot – Firearm
Camp	1	Unfortified camp
Total	9 BGs	Camp, 16 mounted bases, 37 foot bases, 3 commanders

Abbasid standard bearer (centre), by Angus McBride. Taken from Men-at-Arms 125: The Armies of Islam 7th–11th Centuries.

BUILDING A CUSTOMISED LIST USING OUR ARMY POINTS

Choose an army based on the maxima and minima in the list below. The following special instructions apply to this army:

- Commanders should be depicted as Arab, Khurasanian armoured or Turkish *ghilman* cavalry.
- The minimum marked * only applies before 794.
- The minimum marked ** only applies before 836.
- Arab cavalry can always dismount as Heavy Foot, Superior, Average or Poor (as per their mounted class), Undrilled, Armoured, - , Defensive Spearmen.

- *Ghilman* can always dismount as Superior, Armoured, Drilled Medium Foot – Bow, Swordsmen.
- All Zanj and black slave soldier HF must have the same close combat capabilities.
- Berbers cannot be used with Turkish *ghilman*, Dailami or city militia.
- Tulunid or Ikhshidid armies cannot use "Arab cavalry", Khurasanians, Undrilled spearmen and archers, Maghariba and other guards or Dailami.

Arab Cavalry

ABBASID ARAB

Territory Types: Agricultural, Developed, Hilly, Mountains

C–in–C		Inspired Commander/Field Commander/Troop Commander					80/50/35		1	
Sub–commanders		Field Commander					50		0–2	
		Troop Commander					35		0–3	
Troop name		Troop Type				Capabilities		Points per base	Bases per BG	Total bases	
		Type	Armour	Quality	Training	Shooting	Close Combat				
Core Troops											
Arab cavalry	Only before 836	Cavalry	Armoured	Superior	Undrilled	–	Lancers, Swordsmen	16	4–6	*8–32	8–32
				Superior	Drilled			17			
	Only before 874	Cavalry	Armoured	Average	Undrilled	–	Lancers, Swordsmen	12			
				Average	Drilled			13			
	Any date	Cavalry	Armoured	Poor	Undrilled	–	Lancers, Swordsmen	9			
				Poor	Drilled			10			
Khurasanian armoured cavalry	Only from 794 to 835	Cavalry	Armoured	Superior	Undrilled	Bow	Swordsmen	18	4–6	0–12	
Turkish ghilman	Only from 815 to 835	Cavalry	Armoured	Superior	Drilled	Bow	Swordsmen	19	4–6	0–8	
	Only from 836									8–28	
Spearmen and archers	Only before 836	Heavy Foot	Protected	Average	Undrilled	–	Defensive Spearmen	6	2/3	9–12	**12–36
		Light Foot	Unprotected	Average	Undrilled	Bow	–	5	1/3		
	Any date	Heavy Foot	Protected	Poor	Undrilled	–	Defensive Spearmen	4	2/3	9–12	12–36
		Light Foot	Unprotected	Poor	Undrilled	Bow	–	3	1/3		
Maghariba and other guard infantry	Only from 836	Heavy Foot	Protected	Average	Drilled	–	Defensive Spearmen	7	2/3	9–12	0–12
		Light Foot	Unprotected	Average	Drilled	Bow	–	5	1/3		
Zanj and black slave soldiers	Only from 874	Heavy Foot	Protected	Average	Drilled	–	Light Spear, Swordsmen	7	2/3	9–12	9–36
		Heavy Foot	Protected	Average	Drilled	–	Defensive Spearmen	7			
		Light Foot	Unprotected	Average	Drilled	Bow	–	5	1/3		

Troop name		Type	Armour	Quality	Training	Shooting	Close Combat	Points per base	Bases per BG	Total bases
Separately deployed archers		Medium Foot	Protected	Average	Undrilled	Bow	–	6	6–8	0–8
				Poor				4		
		Light Foot	Unprotected	Average	Undrilled	Bow	–	5	6–8	
				Poor				3		
Optional Troops										
Bedouin or volunteer cavalry		Light Horse	Unprotected	Average	Undrilled	–	Lancers, Swordsmen	8	4–6	0–12
		Cavalry	Unprotected	Average	Undrilled	–	Lancers, Swordsmen	8	4–6	
			Protected					9		
Khurasanian light horse archers	Only before 874	Light Horse	Unprotected	Average	Undrilled	Bow	–	8	4–6	0–6
Dailami		Medium Foot	Protected	Superior	Drilled	–	Impact foot, Swordsmen	10	2/3 or all	0–9
			Armoured					13	6–9	
		Light Foot	Unprotected	Superior	Drilled	Bow	–	6	1/3 or 0	
Volunteer foot		Medium Foot	Protected	Superior	Undrilled	–	Impact foot, Swordsmen	9	6–8	0–8
City militia		Mob	Unprotected	Poor	Undrilled	–	–	2	6–8	0–8
Berber light horse	Only before 820	Light Horse	Unprotected	Average	Undrilled	Javelins	Light Spear	7	4–6	0–12
Berber javelinmen	Only before 820	Light Foot	Unprotected	Average	Undrilled	Javelins	Light Spear	4	6–8	0–16
Naffatun		Light Foot	Unprotected	Average	Undrilled	Firearm	–	4	4	0–4
			Protected					5		
Fortified Camp								24		0–1
Allies										
Hamdanid allies (Only from 890) – Bedouin Dynasties										

ABBASID ARAB ALLIES

Allied commander		Field Commander/Troop Commander						40/25		1
Troop name		**Troop Type**				**Capabilities**		**Points per base**	**Bases per BG**	**Total bases**
		Type	Armour	Quality	Training	Shooting	Close Combat			
Arab cavalry	Only before 836	Cavalry	Armoured	Superior	Undrilled	–	Lancers, Swordsmen	16	4–6	0–12
				Superior	Drilled			17		
	Only before 874	Cavalry	Armoured	Average	Undrilled	–	Lancers, Swordsmen	12		4–12
				Average	Drilled			13		
	Any date	Cavalry	Armoured	Poor	Undrilled	–	Lancers, Swordsmen	9		
				Poor	Drilled			10		
Khurasanian armoured cavalry	Only from 794 to 835	Cavalry	Armoured	Superior	Undrilled	Bow	Swordsmen	18	4	0–4
Turkish ghilman	Only from 815	Cavalry	Armoured	Superior	Drilled	Bow	Swordsmen	19	4–6	0–6
Spearmen and archers	Only before 836	Heavy Foot	Protected	Average	Undrilled	–	Defensive Spearmen	6	2/3	6–12
		Light Foot	Unprotected	Average	Undrilled	Bow	–	5	1/3	
	Any date	Heavy Foot	Protected	Poor	Undrilled	–	Defensive Spearmen	4	2/3	6–12
		Light Foot	Unprotected	Poor	Undrilled	Bow	–	3	1/3	6–12
Zanj and black slave soldiers	Only from 874	Heavy Foot	Protected	Average	Drilled	–	Light Spear, Swordsmen	7	2/3	6–12
		Heavy Foot	Protected	Average	Drilled	–	Defensive Spearmen	7		
		Light Foot	Unprotected	Average	Drilled	Bow	–	5	1/3	

Abbasid soldiers, by Graham Turner. Taken from Men-at-Arms 320: Armies of the Caliphates 862–1098.

EARLY NORTH AFRICAN DYNASTIES

This list covers the armies of the North African emirates, from their assumption of independence from the Abbasid Caliphate until the rise of the Murabits. The Idrisids formed their own rival Shiite caliphate in Morocco in 789 which lasted until about 926. The Aghlabids in Tunisia achieved de facto independence by about 820. They subsequently conquered Sicily, which they held until conquered by the Normans between 1060 and 1091.

The Shiite Fatimids replaced the Aghlabids in Tunisia in 909 and this list represents their army from this date until their Egyptian state started to employ Turks and Dailami c.978, after which the Fatimid Egyptian list in Field of Glory Companion 4: *Swords and Scimitars* should be used. After the Fatimid conquest of Egypt, the Zirid dynasty ruled Tunisia as their clients from 972. They were finally conquered by the Almohades c.1160. The Maghrawanids ruled Morocco from the early 11th century until about 1064 when they were conquered by the Murabits.

TROOP NOTES

Armies were based around converted (albeit initially only nominally) Berber tribesmen fighting in a similar style to the Arabs, although the Aghlabids, Fatimids and Zirids also recruited black slave troops as guards and to provide a standing army.

Arab Lancers

EARLY NORTH AFRICAN DYNASTIES (AGHLABID) STARTER ARMY		
Commander-in-Chief	1	Field Commander
Sub-commanders	2	2 x Troop Commander
Arab or Berber lancers	3 BGs	Each comprising 4 bases of Arab or Berber lancers: Superior, Armoured, Undrilled Cavalry – Lancers, Swordsmen
Berber light horse	3 BGs	Each comprising 4 bases of Berber light horse: Average, Unprotected, Undrilled Light Horse – Javelins, Light Spear
Berber spearmen and archers	3 BGs	Each comprising 9 bases of spearmen and archers: 6 Average, Protected, Undrilled Heavy Foot – Defensive Spearmen, 3 Average, Unprotected, Undrilled Light Foot - Bow
Berber javelinmen	2 BGs	Each comprising 6 bases of Berber javelinmen: Average, Unprotected, Undrilled Light Foot – Javelins, Light Spear
Camp	1	Unfortified camp
Total	11 BGs	Camp, 24 mounted bases, 39 foot bases, 3 commanders

BUILDING A CUSTOMISED LIST USING OUR ARMY POINTS

Choose an army based on the maxima and minima in the list below. The following special instructions apply to this army:

- Commanders should be depicted as Arab or Berber lancers.
- All black slave HF must have the same close combat capabilities.

Berber Lancer

EARLY NORTH AFRICAN DYNASTIES

Territory Types: Agricultural, Hilly, Steppes

C–in–C	Inspired Commander/Field Commander/Troop Commander						80/50/35	1	
Sub–commanders	Field Commander						50	0–2	
	Troop Commander						35	0–3	
Troop name	Troop Type				Capabilities		Points per base	Bases per BG	Total bases
	Type	Armour	Quality	Training	Shooting	Close Combat			
Core Troops									
Arab or Berber lancers	Cavalry	Armoured	Superior	Undrilled	–	Lancers, Swordsmen	16	4–6	6–32
		Armoured	Average				12		
		Armoured	Poor				9		
		Protected	Superior				12		
		Protected	Average				9		
		Protected	Poor				7		
Berber light horse	Light Horse	Unprotected	Average	Undrilled	Javelins	Light Spear	7	4–6	12–42
Berber spearmen and archers	Heavy Foot	Protected	Average	Undrilled	–	Defensive Spearmen	6	2/3 9–12	0–36
	Light Foot	Unprotected	Average	Undrilled	Bow	–	5	1/3	
	Heavy Foot	Protected	Poor	Undrilled	–	Defensive Spearmen	4	2/3 9–12	12–36
	Light Foot	Unprotected	Poor	Undrilled	Bow	–	3	1/3	
Black slave javelinmen or spearmen and archers / Only Aghlabids, Fatimids or Zirids	Heavy Foot	Protected	Average	Drilled	–	Light Spear, Swordsmen	7	2/3 9–12	0–24
	Heavy Foot	Protected	Average	Drilled	–	Defensive Spearmen	7		
	Light Foot	Unprotected	Average	Drilled	Bow	–	5	1/3	
Separately deployed archers	Medium Foot	Protected	Average	Undrilled	Bow	–	6	6–8	0–8
			Poor				4		
	Light Foot	Unprotected	Average	Undrilled	Bow	–	5	6–8	
			Poor				3		
Optional Troops									
Berber javelinmen	Light Foot	Unprotected	Average	Undrilled	Javelins	Light Spear	4	6–8	0–16
	Medium Foot	Protected	Average	Undrilled	–	Light Spear	5	6–8	
Berber slingers	Light Foot	Unprotected	Average	Undrilled	Sling	–	4	4–6	0–6
Fortified camp							24		0–1
Allies									
Only outside Sicily									
Tuareg allies (Only from 1000) – See Note p.78									
Only in Sicily (Aghlabids)									
Andalusian allies (Only in 827) – See Field of Glory Companion 8: *Wolves From the Sea: The Dark Ages*									
Byzantine allies (Only in 1035) – Nikephorian Byzantine									
Zirid allies (Only in 1035 or 1063) – Early North African Dynasties									

North African soldiers (foreground) and Bedouin auxiliary (rear), by Angus McBride. Taken from
Men-at-Arms 125: The Armies of Islam 7th–11th Centuries.

EARLY NORTH AFRICAN DYNASTIES ALLIES

Allied commander		Field Commander/Troop Commander					40/25		1	
Troop name		Troop Type				Capabilities		Points per base	Bases per BG	Total bases
		Type	Armour	Quality	Training	Shooting	Close Combat			
Arab or Berber lancers		Cavalry	Armoured	Superior	Undrilled	–	Lancers, Swordsmen	16	4–6	4–12
Arab or Berber lancers		Cavalry	Armoured	Average	Undrilled	–	Lancers, Swordsmen	12	4–6	4–12
Arab or Berber lancers		Cavalry	Armoured	Poor	Undrilled	–	Lancers, Swordsmen	9	4–6	4–12
Berber light horse		Light Horse	Unprotected	Average	Undrilled	Javelins	Light Spear	7	4–6	4–12
Berber spearmen and archers		Heavy Foot	Protected	Average	Undrilled	–	Defensive Spearmen	6	2/3 6–12	0–12 6–12
Berber spearmen and archers		Light Foot	Unprotected	Average	Undrilled	Bow	–	5	1/3	0–12 6–12
Berber spearmen and archers		Heavy Foot	Protected	Poor	Undrilled	–	Defensive Spearmen	4	2/3 6–12	0–12 6–12
Berber spearmen and archers		Light Foot	Unprotected	Poor	Undrilled	Bow	–	3	1/3	0–12 6–12
Black slave javelinmen or spearmen and archers	Only Aghlabids, Fatimids or Zirids	Heavy Foot	Protected	Average	Drilled	–	Light Spear, Swordsmen	7	2/3 6–9	0–9
Black slave javelinmen or spearmen and archers	Only Aghlabids, Fatimids or Zirids	Heavy Foot	Protected	Average	Drilled	–	Defensive Spearmen	7	2/3 6–9	0–9
Black slave javelinmen or spearmen and archers	Only Aghlabids, Fatimids or Zirids	Light Foot	Unprotected	Average	Drilled	Bow	–	5	1/3	0–9

KHURASANIAN DYNASTIES

This list covers the Tahirid (821–873), Saffarid (861–1003) and Samanid (875–999) dynasties in the eastern provinces of the former Abbasid Empire.

The Tahirids rose to power after Tahir ibn Husayn led al-Ma'mun's army to victory in the Abbasid civil war. As a result of this he was made governor of Khurasan, a position which became hereditary following the appointment of his son when he died. Although effectively independent, the Tahirids remained loyal to the Abbasid caliphs and were often given the administration of Baghdad during the period when Samarra became the caliph's residence. They were overthrown by the Saffarids in 873.

The Saffarids started as leaders of brigands and 'Alid secessionists

Volunteer Foot Officer

but rose to conquer the province of Seistan in eastern Persia and to later take over the Tahirid provinces of Khurasan. However, their period of power was short, losing most of their territory to the Samanids in the early 10th century. Even then they survived in Seistan long after the above period as vassals of first the Samanids, then the Ghaznavids, and finally the Seljuqs.

The Samanids were the most successful of the Khurasanian dynasties. Descended from a Persian family they presided over a renaissance of Persian tradition although they remained staunchly Muslim. They fell to the expanding power of the Ghaznavids under Mahmud the Great.

TROOP NOTES

Khurasanian armies relied heavily on the local *Dihqan* class of landowners fighting in a style similar to that of their Sassanid forebears. However, the Saffarids and Samanids, particularly the latter, also recruited Turkish *ghilman* in large numbers.

KHURASANIAN DYNASTIES (SAMANID) STARTER ARMY

Commander-in-Chief	1	Field Commander
Sub-commanders	2	2 x Troop Commander
Turkish ghilman	2 BGs	Each comprising 4 bases of Turkish ghilman: Superior, Armoured, Drilled Cavalry – Bow, Swordsmen
Khurasanian armoured cavalry	2 BGs	Each comprising 4 bases of Khurasanian armoured cavalry: Superior, Armoured, Undrilled Cavalry – Bow, Swordsmen
Khurasanian light horse archers	3 BGs	Each comprising 4 bases of Khurasanian light horse archers: Average, Unprotected, Undrilled Light Horse – Bow
Spearmen and archers	1 BG	12 bases of spearmen and archers: 8 Poor, Protected, Undrilled Heavy Foot – Defensive Spearmen, 4 Poor, Unprotected, Undrilled Light Foot – Bow
Separately deployed archers	1 BG	8 bases of archers: Average, Unprotected, Undrilled Light Foot – Bow
Camp	1	Unfortified camp
Total	9 BGs	Camp, 28 mounted bases, 20 foot bases, 3 commanders

BUILDING A CUSTOMISED LIST USING OUR ARMY POINTS

Choose an army based on the maxima and minima in the list below. The following special instructions apply to this army:

- Commanders should be depicted as Khurasanian armoured cavalry or Turkish *ghilman*.
- *Ghilman* can always dismount as Superior, Armoured, Drilled Medium Foot – Bow, Swordsmen.

KHURASANIAN DYNASTIES

Territory Types: Agricultural, Steppe

C–in–C	Inspired Commander/Field Commander/Troop Commander						80/50/35		1	
Sub–commanders	Field Commander						50		0–2	
	Troop Commander						35		0–3	
Troop name	Troop Type				Capabilities		Points per base	Bases per BG	Total bases	
	Type	Armour	Quality	Training	Shooting	Close Combat				
Core Troops										
Khurasanian armoured cavalry	Cavalry	Armoured	Superior	Undrilled	Bow	Swordsmen	18	4–6	4–18	8–28
Turkish ghilman / Only Samanids or Saffarids	Cavalry	Armoured	Superior	Drilled	Bow	Swordsmen	19	4–6	4–18	
Spearmen and archers	Heavy Foot	Armoured	Average	Undrilled	–	Defensive Spearmen	8	2/3 9–12	9–24	
		Protected					6			
	Light Foot	Unprotected	Average	Undrilled	Bow	–	5	1/3		
	Heavy Foot	Protected	Poor	Undrilled	–	Defensive Spearmen	4	2/3 9–12		
	Light Foot	Unprotected	Poor	Undrilled	Bow	–	3	1/3		
Separately deployed archers	Medium Foot	Protected	Average	Undrilled	Bow	–	6	6–8	0–8	
			Poor				4			
	Light Foot	Unprotected	Average	Undrilled	Bow	–	5			
			Poor				3			
Optional Troops										
Khurasanian light horse archers	Light Horse	Unprotected	Average	Undrilled	Bow	–	8	4–6	0–12	
Turkish mercenary cavalry	Light Horse	Unprotected	Average	Undrilled	Bow	Swordsmen	10	4–6	0–6	
	Cavalry	Unprotected	Average	Undrilled	Bow	Swordsmen	10			
		Protected					11			

Troop name		Type	Armour	Quality	Training	Shooting	Close Combat	Points per base	Bases per BG	Total bases
Bedouin or volunteer cavalry		Light Horse	Unprotected	Average	Undrilled	–	Lancers, Swordsmen	8	4–6	0–12
		Cavalry	Unprotected	Average	Undrilled	–	Lancers, Swordsmen	8	4–6	
			Protected					9		
Dailami		Medium Foot	Protected	Superior	Drilled	–	Impact foot, Swordsmen	10	2/3 or all	0–9
			Armoured					13	6–9	
		Light Foot	Unprotected	Superior	Drilled	Bow	–	6	1/3 or 0	
Volunteer foot		Medium Foot	Protected	Superior	Undrilled	–	Impact foot, Swordsmen	9	6–8	0–8
Hillmen		Medium Foot	Protected	Average	Undrilled	–	Light Spear	5	4–6	0–6
Levy foot		Mob	Unprotected	Poor	Undrilled	–	–	2	6–8	0–8
Elephants	Only Samanids or Saffarids	Elephants	–	Average	–	–	–	25	2	0–2
Fortified camp								24		0–1
Allies										
Only Tahirids										
Abbasid allies										
Only Samanids										
Ghaznavid allies										
Turkish allies – Western Turkish										
Ziyarid allies – Dailami Dynasties										

KHURASANIAN DYNASTIES ALLIES

Allied commander	Field Commander/Troop Commander						40/25		1	
Troop name	Troop Type				Capabilities		Points per base	Bases per BG	Total bases	
	Type	Armour	Quality	Training	Shooting	Close Combat				
Khurasanian armoured cavalry	Cavalry	Armoured	Superior	Undrilled	Bow	Swordsmen	18	4–6	0–6	4–8
Turkish ghilman	Cavalry	Armoured	Superior	Drilled	Bow	Swordsmen	19	4–6	0–6	
Spearmen and archers	Heavy Foot	Armoured	Average	Undrilled	–	Defensive Spearmen	8	2/3	6–9	0–9
		Protected					6			
	Light Foot	Unprotected	Average	Undrilled	Bow	–	5	1/3		
	Heavy Foot	Protected	Poor	Undrilled	–	Defensive Spearmen	4	2/3	6–9	
	Light Foot	Unprotected	Poor	Undrilled	Bow	–	3	1/3		
Khurasanian light horse archers	Light Horse	Unprotected	Average	Undrilled	Bow	–	8	4	0–4	
Bedouin or volunteer cavalry	Light Horse	Unprotected	Average	Undrilled	–	Lancers, Swordsmen	8	4	0–4	
	Cavalry	Unprotected	Average	Undrilled	–	Lancers, Swordsmen	8	4		
		Protected					9			

BEDOUIN DYNASTIES

This list covers the local Arab dynasties in Syria and Iraq that flourished during and after the disintegration of Abbasid power. The main dynasties were the Hamdanids in Mosul (890–991) and Aleppo (944–1008), the Iqaylids in Mosul (996–1096), the Mazyadids in southern Iraq (997–1150) and the Mirdassids in Aleppo (1008–1079), although other minor dynasties and tribes were influential on a smaller scale.

The Hamdanids of the Banu Taghlib were by far the most successful, dominating Mosul, the Jazira (northern Mesopotamia) and northern Syria from the late 9th century onwards, although it wasn't until 905 that one of the family was appointed governor of Mosul and they subsequently consolidated their position. The Mosul branch of the family remained in power, more or less, in Mosul and the surrounding area

Bedouin Cavalry

until 991 when the Iqaylids ousted them. The Aleppo branch was founded by the famous Sayf al-Dawla in 944 when he took over the city with the help of tribesmen of the Banu Kilab, on whom his dynasty politically relied until it fell in 1008, although it had been ineffective since at least 965.

For 20 years following his seizure of power in Aleppo, Sayf al-Dawla was the darling of the Muslim world as he undertook regular raids against the Christian Byzantines, fulfilling the Muslim requirement of *jihad* against non-believers. This also provided an opportunity for others to do so; the city of Tarsus on the border had accommodation for *ghazis* and was a regular starting point for Sayf's raids. However, his credibility fell off as the Byzantines under the Phokas family started to conquer Muslim territory from the mid-century onwards.

TROOP NOTES

Hamdanid armies, unlike the other dynasties, did not rely politically on Bedouin tribesmen but on Turkish *ghilman* and Dailami infantry, the upkeep of which forced them to levy high rates of tax on their subjects.

The armament of the Khurasanian *ghazis* is speculative.

BEDOUIN DYNASTIES (HAMDANID) STARTER ARMY		
Commander-in-Chief	1	Field Commander
Sub-commanders	2	2 x Troop Commander
Turkish ghilman	2 BGs	Each comprising 4 bases of Turkish ghilman: Superior, Armoured, Drilled Cavalry – Bow, Swordsmen
Bedouin cavalry	4 BGs	Each comprising 4 bases of Bedouin cavalry: Average, Unprotected, Undrilled Light Horse – Lancers, Swordsmen
Dailami	3 BGs	Each comprising 6 bases of Dailami: 4 Superior, Armoured, Drilled Medium Foot – Impact Foot, Swordsmen, 2 Superior, Unprotected, Drilled Light Foot - Bow
Camp	1	Unfortified camp
Total	9 BGs	Camp, 24 mounted bases, 18 foot bases, 3 commanders

BUILDING A CUSTOMISED LIST USING OUR ARMY POINTS

Choose an army based on the maxima and minima in the list below. The following special instructions apply to this army:

- Commanders should be depicted as armoured cavalry or *ghilman*.
- *Ghilman* can always dismount as Superior, Armoured, Drilled Medium Foot – Bow, Swordsmen.

BEDOUIN DYNASTIES

Territory Types: Agricultural, Developed, Hilly, Steppes

Troop name		Troop Type				Capabilities		Points per base	Bases per BG	Total bases
C–in–C		Inspired Commander/Field Commander/Troop Commander						80/50/35	1	
Sub–commanders		Field Commander						50	0–2	
		Troop Commander						35	0–3	
		Type	Armour	Quality	Training	Shooting	Close Combat			
Core Troops										
Bedouin or Kurdish armoured cavalry		Cavalry	Armoured	Superior	Undrilled	–	Lancers, Swordsmen	16	4–6	0–12
Other Bedouin cavalry		Light Horse	Unprotected	Average	Undrilled	–	Lancers, Swordsmen	8	4–6	16–96
		Cavalry	Unprotected	Average	Undrilled	–	Lancers, Swordsmen	8	4–6	
			Protected					9		
Bedouin archers		Medium Foot	Protected	Average	Undrilled	Bow	–	6	6–8	0–16
			Unprotected					5		
		Light Foot	Unprotected	Average	Undrilled	Bow	–	5	6–8	
Optional Troops										
Bedouin infantry		Medium Foot	Protected	Average	Undrilled	–	Light Spear, Swordsmen	6	6–8	0–8
Bedouin slingers		Light Foot	Unprotected	Average	Undrilled	Sling	–	4	4	0–4
City militia or peasant foot		Mob	Unprotected	Poor	Undrilled	–	–	2	8–12	0–12
Fortified camp								24		0–1
Ghilman	Only Hamdanids	Cavalry	Armoured	Superior	Drilled	Bow	Swordsmen	19	4–6	0–12
Dailami	Only Iqaylids in 997 or Hamdanids	Medium Foot	Protected	Superior	Drilled	–	Impact foot, Swordsmen	10	2/3 or all	6–9	0–18
			Armoured					13		
		Light Foot	Unprotected	Superior	Drilled	Bow	–	6	1/3 or 0	
Tarsus and other volunteer infantry	Only Hamdanids of Aleppo	Heavy Foot	Protected	Average	Undrilled	–	Defensive Spearmen	6	2/3	9–12	0–18
		Light Foot	Unprotected	Average	Undrilled	Bow	–	5	1/3	
		Heavy Foot	Protected	Poor	Undrilled	–	Defensive Spearmen	4	2/3	9–12	
		Light Foot	Unprotected	Poor	Undrilled	Bow	–	3	1/3	
Ghazis	Only Hamdanids of Aleppo	Medium Foot	Protected	Superior	Undrilled	–	Impact foot, Swordsmen	9	6–8	0–12
		Light Horse	Unprotected	Superior	Undrilled	–	Lancers, Swordsmen	10	4–6	
		Cavalry	Unprotected	Superior	Undrilled	–	Lancers, Swordsmen	10	4–6	
			Protected					12		
Special Campaigns										
Hamdanids of Aleppo from 964 to 965										
Khurasanian ghazis		Cavalry	Armoured	Superior	Undrilled	Bow	Swordsmen	18	4–6	0–18
		Light Horse	Unprotected	Average	Undrilled	Bow	–	8	4–6	
Cannot use ghilman										
Allies										
Kurdish allies (Only Iqaylids)										

BEDOUIN DYNASTIES ALLIES								
Allied commander	Field Commander/Troop Commander					40/25	1	
Troop name	Troop Type				Capabilities		Points per base	Bases per BG	Total bases
	Type	Armour	Quality	Training	Shooting	Close Combat			
Bedouin or Kurdish armoured cavalry	Cavalry	Armoured	Superior	Undrilled	–	Lancers, Swordsmen	16	4	0–4
Other Bedouin cavalry	Light Horse	Unprotected	Average	Undrilled	–	Lancers, Swordsmen	8	4–6	6–24
	Cavalry	Unprotected	Average	Undrilled	–	Lancers, Swordsmen	8	4–6	
		Protected					9		
Bedouin archers	Medium Foot	Protected	Average	Undrilled	Bow	–	6	4–6	0–6
		Unprotected					5		
	Light Foot	Unprotected	Average	Undrilled	Bow	–	5	4–6	

DAILAMI DYNASTIES

This list covers the armies of the dynasties from the northern Iranian Caspian Sea provinces of Dailam and Gilan whose people are usually grouped together as Dailamites. Never fully subdued by the Arab conquests they did not convert to Islam until the early 10th century when 'Alid missionaries finally succeeded.

The most important Dailami dynasty was that of the Buwayhids (Buyids). In 934 AD they took power in Fars, the old centre of the Sassanid Empire, whose riches formed the basis of their takeover of most of the Iraqi and Iranian provinces of the decaying Abbasid caliphate. They took Baghdad in 946 and thereafter ruled as a family confederation of emirates until c.1055 when the emirates fell to the Seljuk Turks. Heavily influenced by

Dailami Standard bearer

the Persian past they even gave their most senior member the title *Shahanshah*.

Although they came to power through the strength of their Dailami infantry, the Buwayhids quickly realised that outside of the mountains they needed cavalry support and so recruited Turkish *ghilman* to meet this need. However, these often came into conflict with the Dailami tribesmen and their upkeep was a heavy burden. They may also have occasionally used small numbers of elephants.

The list also covers the Ziyarids in the Caspian provinces of Gorgan and Mazandaran from 928–1043, and the Musafirids in Azerbaijan from 941–984. Unlike the Buwayhids, these dynasties did not use *ghilman* and had to rely on Kurds and Bedouin for cavalry when they needed them.

TROOP NOTES

Dailami infantry were fierce fighters, armed with large shields and two headed "zupin" javelins. They were sought after as mercenaries throughout the Islamic world.

Dailami infantryman (foreground) and Buwayhid cavalryman (mounted), by Angus McBride.
Taken from Men-at-Arms 125: The Armies of Islam 7th–11th Centuries.

DAILAMI DYNASTIES (BUWAYHID) STARTER ARMY

Commander-in-Chief	1	Field Commander
Sub-commanders	2	2 x Troop Commander
Turkish ghilman	2 BGs	Each comprising 4 bases of Turkish ghilman: Superior, Armoured, Drilled Cavalry – Bow, Swordsmen
Bedouin cavalry	2 BGs	Each comprising 4 bases of Bedouin cavalry: Average, Unprotected, Undrilled Light Horse – Lancers, Swordsmen
Dailami	5 BGs	Each comprising 6 bases of Dailami: 4 Superior, Protected, Drilled Medium Foot – Impact Foot, Swordsmen, 2 Superior, Unprotected, Drilled Light Foot - Bow
Camp	1	Unfortified camp
Total	9 BGs	Camp, 16 mounted bases, 30 foot bases, 3 commanders

BUILDING A CUSTOMISED LIST USING OUR ARMY POINTS

Choose an army based on the maxima and minima in the list below. The following special instructions apply to this army:

- Commanders should be depicted as Dailami foot or Turkish ghilman.
- Ghilman can always dismount as Superior, Armoured, Drilled Medium Foot – Bow, Swordsmen.

DAILAMI DYNASTIES

Territory Types: Agricultural, Developed, Hilly, Mountains

C–in–C		Inspired Commander/Field Commander/Troop Commander						80/50/35		1	
Sub–commanders		Field Commander						50		0–2	
		Troop Commander						35		0–3	
Troop name		Troop Type				Capabilities		Points per base	Bases per BG		Total bases
		Type	Armour	Quality	Training	Shooting	Close Combat				
Core Troops											
Turkish ghilman	Only Buwayhids	Cavalry	Armoured	Superior	Drilled	Bow	Swordsmen	19	4–6		0–24
Dailami foot		Medium Foot	Protected	Superior	Drilled	–	Impact foot, Swordsmen	10	2/3 or all	6–9	24–87
			Armoured					13			
		Light Foot	Unprotected	Superior	Drilled	Bow	–	6	1/3 or 0		
		Medium Foot	Protected	Average	Drilled	–	Impact foot, Swordsmen	8	2/3 or all	6–9	
			Armoured					10			
		Light Foot	Unprotected	Average	Drilled	Bow	–	5	1/3 or 0		
Separately deployed Dailami archers		Medium Foot	Protected	Superior	Drilled	Bow	–	9	6–8		0–8
				Average				7			
		Light Foot	Unprotected	Superior	Drilled	Bow	–	6	6–8		
				Average				5			
Optional Troops											
Bedouin cavalry		Light Horse	Unprotected	Average	Undrilled	–	Lancers, Swordsmen	8	4–6		0–8
		Cavalry	Unprotected	Average	Undrilled	–	Lancers, Swordsmen	8	4–6		
			Protected					9			

KURDISH ALLIES

Kurdish cavalry		Cavalry	Armoured	Superior	Undrilled	–	Lancers, Swordsmen	16	4–6	0–6
				Average				12		
Indian Zott mercenaries	Only Buwayhids	Medium Foot	Unprotected	Average	Undrilled	–	Skilled Swordsmen	6	4–6	0–6
Elephants		Elephants	–	Average	–	–	–	25	2	0–2
Fortified camp								24		0–1
Allies										
Bagratid Armenian allies (Only Musafarids)										
Hamdanid or other Bedouin allies (Only Buwayhids) – Bedouin Dynasties										
Kurdish allies										
Saffarid allies (Only Buwayhids) – Khurasanian Dynasties										

DAILAMI DYNASTIES ALLIES

Allied commander		Field Commander/Troop Commander						40/25		1	
Troop name		Troop Type				Capabilities		Points per base	Bases per BG	Total bases	
		Type	Armour	Quality	Training	Shooting	Close Combat				
Dailami foot		Medium Foot	Protected	Superior	Drilled	–	Impact foot, Swordsmen	10	2/3 or all	6–9	6–18
			Armoured					13			
		Light Foot	Unprotected	Superior	Drilled	Bow	–	6	1/3 or 0		
		Medium Foot	Protected	Average	Drilled	–	Impact foot, Swordsmen	8	2/3 or all	6–9	
			Armoured					10			
		Light Foot	Unprotected	Average	Drilled	Bow	–	5	1/3 or 0		

KURDISH ALLIES

- Commanders should be depicted as cavalry

KURDISH ALLIES

Allied commander	Field Commander/Troop Commander						40/25		1
Troop name	Troop Type				Capabilities		Points per base	Bases per BG	Total bases
	Type	Armour	Quality	Training	Shooting	Close Combat			
Cavalry	Cavalry	Armoured	Superior	Undrilled	–	Lancers, Swordsmen	16	4–6	6–12
			Average				12		
Archers	Medium Foot	Unprotected	Average	Undrilled	Bow	–	5	4–6	0–6
	Light Foot	Unprotected	Average	Undrilled	Bow	–	5	4–6	

BAGRATID ARMENIAN ALLIES

- Commanders should be depicted as nobles.

BAGRATID ARMENIAN ALLIES								
Allied commander	Field Commander/Troop Commander						40/25	1
Troop name	Troop Type				Capabilities		Points per base	Bases per BG	Total bases
	Type	Armour	Quality	Training	Shooting	Close Combat			
Nobles and retainers	Cavalry	Armoured	Superior	Undrilled	–	Lancers, Swordsmen	16	4–6	4–6
Skirmishing retainers	Light Horse	Unprotected	Average	Undrilled	Bow	–	8	4–6	4–6
Spearmen and supporting archers	Heavy Foot	Protected	Average	Undrilled	–	Defensive Spearmen	6	2/3 or all	6–12	6–12
	Light Foot	Unprotected	Average	Undrilled	Bow	–	5	1/3 or 0		
	Heavy Foot	Protected	Poor	Undrilled	–	Defensive Spearmen	4	2/3 or all	6–12	
	Light Foot	Unprotected	Poor	Undrilled	Bow	–	3	1/3 or 0		
Separately deployed archers	Light Foot	Unprotected	Average	Undrilled	Bow	–	5	6–8	0–8
			Poor				3		
	Medium Foot	Unprotected	Average	Undrilled	Bow	–	5	6–8	
			Poor				3		

PECHENEG

The Pechenegs (Patzinaks) were a nomadic or semi-nomadic Turkic people who defeated the Magyars in the mid-9th century AD, pushing them westwards, and occupied much of the southwestern Eurasian steppe.

They were commonly used as allies or mercenaries by the Byzantines. They came into frequent conflict with the Rus, besieging Kiev in 968, though they sometimes allied with the Rus against the Byzantines. In 1036 they were decisively defeated by the Rus, following which they were driven from the steppe by the Cumans and migrated to the north bank of the Danube. In 1091 they were severely defeated at Levounion by a combined Byzantine and Cuman army under the Emperor Alexios I Komnenos. They were again defeated by the Cumans in 1094 and

the Byzantines under John II Komnenos at Beroia in 1122. Thereafter they survived only as remnant populations.

This list covers Pecheneg armies from the mid 9th century until their suppression by the Byzantines in 1122.

Pecheneg Heavy Cavalry

PECHENEG STARTER ARMY

Commander-in-Chief	1	Field Commander
Sub-commanders	2	2 x Troop Commander
Heavy cavalry	3 BGs	Each comprising 4 bases of heavy cavalry: Superior, Armoured, Undrilled Cavalry – Bow, Swordsmen
Light cavalry	6 BGs	Each comprising 4 bases of light cavalry: Average, Unprotected, Undrilled Light Horse – Bow, Swordsmen
Camp	1	Fortified camp
Total	9 BGs	Fortified camp, 36 mounted bases, 3 commanders

BUILDING A CUSTOMISED LIST USING OUR ARMY POINTS

Choose an army based on the maxima and minima in the list below. The following special instructions apply to this army:

- Commanders should be depicted as heavy cavalry.

PECHENEG

Territory Types: Steppes									
C–in–C	Inspired Commander/Field Commander/Troop Commander						80/50/35	1	
Sub–commanders	Field Commander						50	0–2	
	Troop Commander						35	0–3	
Troop name	Troop Type				Capabilities		Points per base	Bases per BG	Total bases
	Type	Armour	Quality	Training	Shooting	Close Combat			
Core Troops									
Heavy cavalry	Cavalry	Armoured	Superior	Undrilled	Bow	Swordsmen	18	4–6	0–12
Light cavalry	Light Horse	Unprotected	Average	Undrilled	Bow	Swordsmen	10	4–6	24–96
	Cavalry	Unprotected	Average	Undrilled	Bow	Swordsmen	10		
		Protected					11		
Optional Troops									
Fortified camp (wagon laager)							24		0–1

PECHENEG ALLIES

Allied commander	Field Commander/Troop Commander						40/25	1	
Troop name	Troop Type				Capabilities		Points per base	Bases per BG	Total bases
	Type	Armour	Quality	Training	Shooting	Close Combat			
Heavy cavalry	Cavalry	Armoured	Superior	Undrilled	Bow	Swordsmen	18	4	0–4
Light cavalry	Light Horse	Unprotected	Average	Undrilled	Bow	Swordsmen	10	4–6	8–24
	Cavalry	Unprotected	Average	Undrilled	Bow	Swordsmen	10		
		Protected					11		

Pecheneg chieftan (right), by Angus McBride. Taken from Men-at-Arms 333: Armies of Medieval Russia *750–1250.*

GHAZNAVID

This list covers the armies of the Ghaznavid dynasty from 962 AD when Alp Tigin (a Turkic *ghulam* general) acquired power at Ghazna in eastern Afghanistan, until the fall of the dynasty. Alp Tigin's successor Sebük Tigin conquered most of Afghanistan and the Punjab.

From this solid base his son, Mahmud the Great, conquered the remainder of the Samanid territory and much of northern India between 997 and 1024. The final piece of expansion was the acquisition of Rayy from the Buwayhids in 1027, pushing his empire to just south of the Caspian Sea. Mahmud and his successors continued to raid deep into India on a regular basis for the next 140 years, obtaining great booty at the cost of much suffering and slaughter amongst the Indian population. Although held in high regard by Muslims as a *ghazi* (fighter for the faith) he is remembered as a bloody-handed barbarian by Indians.

By the second quarter of the 11th century, however, the empire was under pressure from the rising power of the Seljuk Turks. In 1040, at the Battle of Dandanaqan, Mahmud's son Mas'ud was decisively defeated and nearly all of Khurasan was lost. Following this the Ghurids, an Afghan dynasty, rebelled and pushed the Ghaznavids back to their Indian possessions. The last territories, in Lahore, fell to the Ghurids in 1187.

TROOP NOTES

Ghaznavid armies were noted for their use of elephants, which were obtained as a result of the massive raids into India. Numbers such as 1,300 and 1,670 are mentioned as being present at military reviews. The elephants were normally armoured.

Naffatun were armed with naphtha bombs – the medieval equivalent of Molotov cocktails.

Ghazanavid warrior, by Graham Turner. Taken from Men-at-Arms 320: Armies of the Caliphates 862–1098.

BUILDING A CUSTOMISED LIST USING OUR ARMY POINTS

Choose an army based on the maxima and minima in the list below. The following special instructions apply to this army:

- Commanders should be depicted as *ghilman* or elephants.
- *Ghilman* can always dismount as Superior, Armoured, Drilled Medium Foot – Bow, Swordsmen.
- Only one allied contingent can be used.
- Indian allies cannot be used with Dailami, Arabs or Kurds.

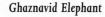

Ghaznavid Elephant

GHAZNAVID STARTER ARMY		
Commander-in-Chief	1	Field Commander
Sub-commanders	2	2 x Troop Commander
Ghilman	3 BGs	Each comprising 4 bases of Ghilman: Superior, Armoured, Drilled Cavalry – Bow, Swordsmen
Nomad horse archers	2 BGs	Each comprising 4 bases of nomad horse archers: Average, Unprotected, Undrilled Light Horse – Bow, Swordsmen
Arab volunteer cavalry	1 BG	4 bases of Arab volunteer cavalry: Average, Unprotected, Undrilled Light Horse – Lancers, Swordsmen
Elephants	2 BGs	Each comprising 2 bases of elephants: Average, Undrilled Elephants
Separately deployed archers	1 BG	8 bases of archers: Poor, Unprotected, Undrilled Light Foot – Bow
Naffatun	1 BG	4 bases of naffatun: Average, Unprotected, Undrilled Light Foot – Firearm
Camp	1	Unfortified camp
Total	10 BGs	Camp, 28 mounted bases, 12 foot bases, 3 commanders

GHAZNAVID

Territory Types: Agricultural, Hilly, Steppes

C–in–C	Inspired Commander/Field Commander/Troop Commander					80/50/35	1	
Sub–commanders	Field Commander					50	0–2	
	Troop Commander					35	0–3	

Troop name	Troop Type				Capabilities		Points per base	Bases per BG	Total bases
	Type	Armour	Quality	Training	Shooting	Close Combat			
Core Troops									
Ghilman	Cavalry	Armoured	Superior	Drilled	Bow	Swordsmen	19	4–6	8–24
Nomad horse archers	Light Horse	Unprotected	Average	Undrilled	Bow	Swordsmen	10	4–6	4–12
	Cavalry	Unprotected	Average	Undrilled	Bow	Swordsmen	10		
		Protected					11		
Optional Troops									
Elephants	Elephants	–	Average	–	–	–	25	2	0–8
Arab or Kurdish armoured cavalry	Cavalry	Armoured	Superior	Undrilled	–	Lancers, Swordsmen	16	4–6	0–6
			Average				12		
Arab volunteer cavalry	Light Horse	Unprotected	Average	Undrilled	–	Lancers, Swordsmen	8	4–6	0–6
	Cavalry	Unprotected	Average	Undrilled	–	Lancers, Swordsmen	8	4–6	
		Protected					9		
Spearmen and supporting archers	Heavy Foot	Armoured	Average	Undrilled	–	Defensive Spearmen	8	2/3	6–12	0–12	0–12
		Protected					6		
	Light Foot	Unprotected	Average	Undrilled	Bow	–	5	1/3	
	Heavy Foot	Protected	Poor	Undrilled	–	Defensive Spearmen	4	2/3	6–12	
	Light Foot	Unprotected	Poor	Undrilled	Bow	–	3	1/3	
Separately deployed archers	Medium Foot	Protected	Average	Undrilled	Bow	–	6	6–8	0–8
			Poor				4		
	Light Foot	Unprotected	Average	Undrilled	Bow	–	5		
			Poor				3		
Dailami	Medium Foot	Protected	Superior	Drilled	–	Impact foot, Swordsmen	10	2/3 or all	6–9	0–9
		Armoured					13		
	Light Foot	Unprotected	Superior	Drilled	Bow	–	6	1/3 or 0	
Ghazi foot	Medium Foot	Protected	Superior	Undrilled	–	Impact foot, Swordsmen	9	4–6	0–6
Afghan spearmen	Medium Foot	Protected	Average	Undrilled	–	Light Spear	5	4–6	0–6
Indian or Afghan archers	Medium Foot	Unprotected	Average	Undrilled	Bow	–	5	6–8	0–8
Naffatun	Light Foot	Unprotected	Average	Undrilled	Firearm	–	4	4	0–4
		Protected					5		
Stone throwers	Heavy Artillery	–	Average	–	Heavy Artillery	–	20	2	0–2
Field fortifications	Field Fortifications						3		0–12
Fortified camp							24		0–1
Allies									
Indian allies – Hindu Indian See Note p.78									
Qarakhanid allies – See Note p.78									

NIKEPHORIAN BYZANTINE

Under the Macedonian dynasty (867–1056 AD) the Byzantine Empire was once again strong enough to go on the offensive. Initially the attempted reconquest met with mixed success. However, the soldier emperors Nikephoros II Phokas (963–969) and John I Tzimiskes (969–976) reconquered Crete, Cyprus and parts of Syria. Basil II (976–1025) conquered the Bulgar Empire after a campaign lasting nearly twenty years. The Bulgars finally surrendered in 1018 and were incorporated into the empire, restoring the Danube frontier last held 400 years before.

Following the death of Basil II, the civil service faction gained the upper hand, reducing the expensive native army and relying more on short-term mercenary contracts. The Normans conquered the last Byzantine possessions in Italy.

Nikephorian Kataphraktoi

In 1071, the main Byzantine field army, under the Emperor Romanus IV Diogenes, was decisively defeated by the Seljuk Turks under Sultan Alp Arslan at Manzikert in Asia Minor. Over the next few years most of Asia Minor was lost to the Turks.

This list covers Byzantine armies from 963 until 1071.

TROOP NOTES

The army declined in the latter part of the period, mainly due to cost cutting by the central bureaucracy, and archery became uncommon among the regular cavalry.

The *kataphraktoi* formed in one or occasionally two deep wedges, designed to break into the enemy army.

The Varangian guard in this period were armed with spears, axes only becoming their main weapon later – probably following the influx of English recruits after the Norman conquest of England.

NIKEPHORIAN BYZANTINE

Byzantine Klibanophoros, by Angus McBride. Taken from Men-at-Arms 89: Byzantine Armies 886–1118.

NIKEPHORIAN BYZANTINE STARTER ARMY		
Commander-in-Chief	1	Field Commander
Sub-commanders	2	2 x Troop Commander
Cavalry	2 BGs	Each comprising 4 bases of cavalry: Superior, Armoured, Drilled Cavalry – Bow*, Lancers, Swordsmen
Kataphraktoi	1 BG	2 bases of kataphraktoi: Elite, Heavily Armoured, Drilled Cataphracts – 1 Lancers, Swordsmen, 1 Bow, Swordsmen
Flankers	2 BGs	Each comprising 4 bases of flankers: Average, Protected, Drilled Cavalry – Bow, Swordsmen
Spearmen and archers	2 BGs	Each comprising 8 bases of spearmen and archers: 4 Average, Protected, Drilled Heavy Foot – Defensive Spearmen, 4 Average, Protected, Drilled Medium Foot – Bow
Rus mercenaries	1 BG	6 bases of Rus mercenaries: Average, Protected, Undrilled Heavy Foot – Offensive Spearmen
Skirmishing archers	1 BG	8 bases of archers: Poor, Unprotected, Drilled Light Foot – Bow
Camp	1	Unfortified camp
Total	9 BGs	Camp, 18 mounted bases, 30 foot bases, 3 commanders

BUILDING A CUSTOMISED LIST USING OUR ARMY POINTS

Choose an army based on the maxima and minima in the list below. The following special instructions apply to this army:

- Commanders should be depicted as cavalry or (one) as Norman mercenaries.
- *Kataphraktoi* bowmen shoot as if cavalry.
- The minimum marked * only applies if the Emperor is present.

- Minima marked ** only apply if any foot are used.

Nikephorian
Cavalry

NIKEPHORIAN BYZANTINE								
Territory Types: Agricultural, Developed, Hilly, Mountains								
C–in–C	Inspired Commander/Field Commander/Troop Commander						80/50/35	1
Sub–commanders	Field Commander						50	0–2
	Troop Commander						35	0–3
Troop name	Troop Type				Capabilities		Points per base	Bases per BG	Total bases
	Type	Armour	Quality	Training	Shooting	Close Combat			
Core Troops									
Cavalry	Before 1042	Cavalry	Armoured	Superior	Drilled	Bow*	Lancers, Swordsmen	19	4–6	6–26
	From 1042								4–6	0–6
	From 1042	Cavalry	Armoured	Average	Drilled	–	Lancers, Swordsmen	13	4–6	6–18
			Protected					10		
Kataphraktoi		Cataphracts	Heavily Armoured	Elite	Drilled	–	Lancers, Swordsmen	23	1/2	2	0–4
		Cataphracts	Heavily Armoured	Elite	Drilled	Bow	Swordsmen	25	1/2		
		Cataphracts	Heavily Armoured	Superior	Drilled	–	Lancers, Swordsmen	20	1/2	2	
		Cataphracts	Heavily Armoured	Superior	Drilled	Bow	Swordsmen	22	1/2		
Flankers		Cavalry	Protected	Average	Drilled	Bow	Swordsmen	12	4	0–8
Varangian guard	Only from 1042	Heavy Foot	Heavily Armoured	Elite	Drilled	–	Offensive Spearmen	19	4–6	*4–6
			Heavily Armoured	Superior				16		
			Armoured	Elite				16		
			Armoured	Superior				13		
Spearmen and archers		Heavy Foot	Protected	Average	Drilled	–	Defensive Spearmen	7	1/2	6–8	**12–32
		Medium Foot	Protected	Average	Drilled	Bow	–	7	1/2		
		Heavy Foot	Protected	Poor	Drilled	–	Defensive Spearmen	5	1/2	6–8	
		Medium Foot	Protected	Poor	Drilled	Bow	–	5	1/2		
Skirmishing archers		Light Foot	Unprotected	Average	Drilled	Bow	–	5	6–8	0–12	**6–24
				Poor				3			
Javelinmen		Light Foot	Unprotected	Average	Drilled	Javelins	Light Spear	4	6–8	0–12	
				Poor				2			

Optional Troops									
Detached menavlatoi		Heavy Foot	Protected	Average	Drilled	–	Heavy Weapon	8	4–6	0–6
Slingers		Light Foot	Unprotected	Average	Drilled	Sling	–	4	4–6	0–6
				Poor				2		
Rus or Varangian mercenaries	Only before 1042	Heavy Foot	Protected	Average	Undrilled	–	Offensive Spearmen	7	6–8	0–12
Norman mercenaries	Only from 1042	Knights	Armoured	Superior	Undrilled	–	Lancers, Swordsmen	20	4–6	0–6
Alan, Cuman, Pecheneg or Turkish mercenaries	Only from 1042	Light Horse	Unprotected	Average	Undrilled	Bow	Swordsmen	10	4–6	0–12
		Cavalry	Unprotected	Average	Undrilled	Bow	Swordsmen	10		
			Protected					11		
Bolt–shooters or stone–throwers		Heavy Artillery	–	Average	–	Heavy Artillery	–	20	2	0–2
Fortified camp								24		0–1
Allies										
Armenian allies (Only before 976) – Bagratid Armenian										
Hamdanid allies (Only before 976) – Bedouin Dynasties										
Georgian allies (Only from 977) – See Field of Glory Companion 4: Swords and Scimitars: The Crusades										

NIKEPHORIAN BYZANTINE ALLIES

Allied commander		Field Commander/Troop Commander						40/25	1	
Troop name		Troop Type				Capabilities		Points per base	Bases per BG	Total bases
		Type	Armour	Quality	Training	Shooting	Close Combat			
Cavalry	Before 1042	Cavalry	Armoured	Superior	Drilled	Bow*	Lancers, Swordsmen	19	4–6	4–8
	From 1042	Cavalry	Armoured	Average	Drilled	–	Lancers, Swordsmen	13	4–6	
			Protected					10		
Alan, Cuman, Pecheneg or Turkish mercenaries	Only from 1042	Light Horse	Unprotected	Average	Undrilled	Bow	Swordsmen	10	4	0–4
		Cavalry	Unprotected	Average	Undrilled	Bow	Swordsmen	10		
			Protected					11		
Spearmen and archers		Heavy Foot	Protected	Average	Drilled	–	Defensive Spearmen	7	1/2	6–8	**6–12
		Medium Foot	Protected	Average	Drilled	Bow	–	7	1/2	
		Heavy Foot	Protected	Poor	Drilled	–	Defensive Spearmen	5	1/2	6–8
		Medium Foot	Protected	Poor	Drilled	Bow	–	5	1/2	
Skirmishing archers		Light Foot	Unprotected	Average	Drilled	Bow	–	5	4	0–4
				Poor				3		
Javelinmen		Light Foot	Unprotected	Average	Drilled	Javelins	Light Spear	4	4	0–4
				Poor				2		

APPENDIX 1 – USING THE LISTS

To give balanced games, armies can be selected using the points system. The more effective the troops, the more each base costs in points. The maximum points for an army will usually be set at between 600 and 800 points for a singles game for 2 to 4 hours play. We recommend 800 points for 15mm singles tournament games (650 points for 25mm) and 1000 points for 15mm doubles games.

The army lists specify which troops can be used in a particular army. No other troops can be used. The number of bases of each type in the army must conform to the specified minima and maxima. Troops that have restrictions on when they can be used cannot be used with troops with a conflicting restriction. For example, troops that can only be used "before 638" cannot be used with troops that can only be used "from 638". All special instructions applying to an army list must be adhered to. They also apply to allied contingents supplied by the army.

All armies must have a C-in-C and at least one other commander. No army can have more than 4 commanders in total, including C-in-C, sub-commanders and allied commanders.

All armies must have a supply camp. This is free unless fortified. A fortified camp can only be used if specified in the army list. Field fortifications and portable defences can only be used if specified in the army list.

Allied contingents can only be used if specified in the army list. Most allied contingents have their own allied contingent list, to which they must conform unless the main army's list specifies otherwise.

BATTLE GROUPS

All troops are organized into battle groups. Commanders, supply camps and field fortifications are not troops and are not assigned to battle groups. Portable defences are not troops, but are assigned to specific battle groups.

Battle groups must obey the following restrictions:

- The number of bases in a battle group must correspond to the range specified in the army list.
- Each battle group must initially comprise an even number of bases. The only exception to this rule is that battle groups whose army list specifies them as 2/3 of one type and 1/3 of another, can comprise 9 bases if this is within the battle group size range specified by the list.
- A battle group can only include troops from one line in a list, unless the list specifies a mixed formation by specifying fractions of the battle group to be of types from two lines. e.g. 2/3 spearmen, 1/3 archers.
- All troops in a battle group must be of the same quality and training. When a choice of quality or training is given in a list, this allows battle groups to differ from each other. It does not permit variety within a battle group.
- Unless specifically stated otherwise in an army list, all troops in a battle group must be of the same armour class. When a choice of armour class is given in a list, this allows

battle groups to differ from each other. It does not permit variety within a battle group.

EXAMPLE LIST

Here is a section of an actual army list, which will help us to explain the basics and some special features. The list specifies the following items for each historical type included in the army:

- Troop Type - comprising Type, Armour, Quality and Training.
- Capabilities – comprising Shooting and Close Combat capabilities.
- Points cost per base.
- Minimum and maximum number of bases in each battle group.
- Minimum and maximum number of bases in the army.

Troop name		Troop Type				Capabilities		Points per base	Bases per BG	Total bases
		Type	Armour	Quality	Training	Shooting	Close Combat			
Foot warriors	Before 638	Heavy Foot	Protected	Superior	Undrilled	–	Offensive Spearmen	9	2/3 or all	24–84
	From 638								8–9	12–48
Supporting archers		Light Foot	Unprotected	Superior	Undrilled	Bow	–	6	1/3 or 0	0–24
Separately deployed archers		Medium Foot	Protected	Superior	Undrilled	Bow	–	8	6–8	0–24
				Average				6		
		Light Foot	Unprotected	Superior	Undrilled	Bow	–	6	6–8	0–12
				Average				5		
Jund cavalry	Only from 638	Cavalry	Protected	Superior	Undrilled	–	Lancers, Swordsmen	12	4–6	12–24
				Average				9		

SPECIAL FEATURES:

- Each foot warrior battle group can either be all spearmen or 2/3 spearmen, 1/3 supporting archers. It is permitted for some battle groups to be all spearmen and some to be mixed. If all spearmen, each battle group must be of 8 bases. If mixed, each battle group must be of 9 bases. Before 638 AD, the minimum total number of foot warrior spearmen bases in the army is 24, and the maximum is 84. From 638, the minimum number is 12, and the maximum is 48. The maximum total number of supporting archer bases in the army is 24.
- Separately deployed archers can be fielded as Medium Foot or Light Foot, and can be

of Superior or Average quality. All the bases in a battle group must be classified the same. Each battle group can be of 6 or 8 bases. The maximum total number of bases of separately deployed archers in the army is 12. The maximum combined total number of bases of supporting and separately deployed archers in the army is 24.

- Jund cavalry can only be used from 638 AD. They can be of Superior or Average quality. All the bases in a battle group must be of the same quality. Each battle group can be of 4 or 6 bases. The minimum total number of Jund cavalry bases in the army (from 638) is 12, and the maximum is 24.

APPENDIX 2 – THEMED TOURNAMENTS

A tournament based on the "Byzantium and Islam" theme can include any of the armies listed in this book.

It can also include the following armies from our other army list books. These can only use options permitted between 493 AD and 1071 AD inclusive:

Field of Glory Companion 5: *Legions Triumphant: Imperial Rome at War*

Early Alan

Sassanid Persian

Gepid or Early Lombard

Western Hunnic

Field of Glory Companion 8: *Wolves From the Sea: The Dark Ages*

Magyar

Field of Glory Companion: *Feudal Europe*

(See note below)

Early Hungarian

Field of Glory Companion 4: *Swords and Scimitars: The Crusades*

Fatimid Egyptian

Georgian

Seljuk Turk

Cuman

Note: Some of the army lists referenced in this book are planned either to be included in future *Field of Glory* Companions or as free downloads from the *Field of Glory* website. We have included them in these lists for the sake of historical accuracy. Visit www.fieldofglory.com to keep up-to-date with the latest Companion and army list releases.

INDEX